RIDE THE WAVE

JOHN WESSINGER

RIDE THE WAVE

HOW TO EMBRACE CHANGE AND CREATE A POWERFUL NEW RELATIONSHIP WITH RISK

WISE
CREATIVE ★ PUBLISHING
Ink
2012

Print ISBN 13: 978-1-63489-064-9

Library of Congress Catalog Number: 2017938415

Printed in the United States of America
First Printing: 2017
21 20 19 18 17   5 4 3 2 1

Cover and Interior design by Dan Pitts

Wise Ink Creative Publishing
837 Glenwood Avenue
Minneapolis, MN 55405
wiseinkpub.com

To order, visit itascabooks.com or call 1-800-901-3480.
Reseller discounts available.

ENDORSEMENT

"This is the type of book that anyone passionate about sales and marketing should read. It's personal, it's actionable, and it's well-written."

— ADAM DINCE, author of *Hopeful to Hired*

TABLE OF CONTENTS

"When risk is a challenge, fear becomes a compass – literally pointing people in the direction they need to go. To really achieve anything, you have to be able to tolerate and enjoy risk. In all fields, to make exceptional discoveries you need risk – you're never going to have a breakthrough without it."

—*Barbara Sahakian*
(University of Cambridge Neuropsychologist)

FROM THE AUTHOR

On July 1, 2014, I began a new journey. Much like an odyssey, I answered a call to an adventure that would change how I approached business and my life. My journey was tough. The toughest thing I have ever done. I experienced two epic failures that would serve as the genesis for this book, and the challenges I write about here are ones that I had to overcome personally. I have firsthand experience with everything written in this book and have the mental and physical scars to prove it. In writing this book, I kept specific people in mind and wanted those closest to me to serve as the inspiration and audience for this book. My goal was to entertain, motivate, and forever change the people who would read my story. Even though this is my journey, there's a universal lesson within the pages and chapters of this book and a unique message that will help anyone overcome a new business or personal challenge that is bigger than themselves.

The reason you need to read this book is because of change. Change is happening in business, and it's impacting our personal lives faster than anyone could have predicted or anticipated. We're starting to see the power of technology and information when it's available to anyone with an Internet connection. We've seen how small companies, large organizations, and even individuals are leveraging that power to do amazing things on an unprecedented scale. In order to adapt to this change and stay relevant, you will need the ability to understand, manage, and explore the changing business situations around you quickly and effectively. You will need to ask, "What are the challenges of the new market conditions? What skills or knowledge is needed? What personal and professional risk am I willing to take on to find success?"

During my journey, I answered these questions through a set of personal and professional experiences. These experiences led me to write this book and to create a process to overcome these new challenges for myself, but also for others. I developed this process for anyone to understand and overcome the new challenges happening around them. In this book, I want to share what I learned and help you overcome the same challenges I experienced. This is your playbook for the new way to succeed in business and life.

This book will walk you through a new process for overcoming challenges and give you the confidence to make tough decisions and find success. What makes this book different is the use of the surfer as a model for you to follow and a new set of principles to apply to the business world. These principles create a repeatable process that's simple and easy to use, but that also achieves results. Most books use the past to try to explain the future. This book looks forward, however, instead of looking back, and uses the lens of the surfer to encourage action in a new direction. Riding the wave is about using the natural momentum of the change that we're experiencing to overcome challenges instead of being crushed or wiped out by them. The goal is to be more like the surfer and to *ride the wave*.

SECTION I:
A CALL TO ADVENTURE

"Life should not be a journey to the grave
with the intention of arriving safely in a pretty
and well preserved body, but rather to skid
in broadside in a cloud of smoke, thoroughly
used up, totally worn out, and loudly
proclaiming 'Wow! What a Ride!'"

—*Hunter S. Thompson*

INTRODUCTION: A UNIVERSAL EXPERIENCE

MY PERSONAL JOURNEY

1. I WAS OBSOLETE

MARKET CONDITIONS

I had become obsolete. At least my job felt like it had become obsolete, and since it can be hard to separate our individual selves from our work, the feeling was that I was obsolete and that my job would be much different in the not-so-distant future. I noticed that the market conditions I worked in were also starting to change around me. In the middle of it, it was hard to know what was happening or the true reality of the situation. I felt like I had grown and developed as a professional over the years, holding various organizational roles and receiving an MBA, for example. However, somehow the environment around me had changed almost overnight, and I was left thinking to myself, "What just happened here?"

RESISTANCE MINDSET

After having some level of professional success doing the same thing for so long, it was hard to mentally wrap my mind around the change that was happening. It was really easy to fall back on "the basics" during difficult times or stick to "blocking and tackling" when faced with new challenges. But somehow the traditional methods and skills I had built over the years felt wrong—as though they had no impact on what I was doing. It was also hard to make a change when my organization supported "the old way of doing things." This feeling was not just limited to myself. This change was felt company wide, and as an organization, we really struggled to sell and market our products effectively in this new environment. We developed major marketing and sales initiatives that were well planned, but we were somehow frustrating our customers with what we were doing. They already seemed to have the information and knowledge about our products and services before we rolled out anything new.

AVERSION TO RISK

I knew that I needed to change my mindset about how I approached my role and do something different in response to what was happening around me. However, this process proved to be a lot more challenging given our history of success and also due to the fact that everyone around me was doing the same thing we had always done before. We were using the same strategies, with the same set of skills, but somehow expecting a different or better result. We were beat up mentally and were unwilling to change what we were doing to tackle the risks these new challenges presented. Change was hard because of the risk involved with doing something new. I had to physically stop what I was doing and forget about everything I had done previously that had made me successful because I knew it was no longer going to work. It was risky, but I knew that I had to change in order to move forward or I was going to be left behind.

2. SALES AND MARKETING CHANGED

NEW CONDITIONS

What was happening? Why was I experiencing this change, and was it specific to my profession, company, or industry? The short answer is no. This was something universal that was happening throughout business and that is continuing to happen as more and more disruption takes place because of technology and changing market conditions. These new conditions have given the customer a new level of buying power. There is more access to information, more social sharing platforms, and more channels for customers to seek out and find new ways to buy. As technology and information-sharing platforms continue to drive the new buying process, the challenge for organizations will be keeping up with the change, staying relevant, and meeting the new demands of consumers. Buyers are no longer relying on an organization to help them make a purchase decision, which means that business leaders will need a new set of skills and a fresh mindset to satisfy customer needs.

NEW MINDSET

The market conditions in which companies are operating have changed, and customers are now in the position of power. Organizations no longer have the ability to dictate a sales and marketing process through a traditional "funnel" system. This one-size-fits-all approach is drowning customers with information and is a turnoff to buying a product or service. Customers want to be intrigued and challenged; they want to discover a new product or service on their own. This new customer-decision journey has been supercharged by technology and information-sharing platforms, and it looks as though there is little to slow down the pace of this rapid change any time soon. In fact, this new decision journey only seems to be evolving and moving faster. New skills and capabilities are needed to keep up with this change as well as the new mindset needed to manage it. This new dynamic with customers has left some companies scratching their heads and baffled by the new conditions, struggling to find success, and scrambling to add new skills and capabilities to keep up.

NEW RISK

As a result of these new conditions and the urgent need for new skills, a new relationship with risk has developed. For leadership, there has always been some form of risk involved with business. However, risk was generally something to be avoided, and companies with deep pockets could often bail themselves out of a bad situation if needed. However, the new conditions have changed that dynamic. Risk is now the new norm, and it is also the new path to success. Leaders who are not exploring risk willingly are exposing themselves as well as the organization to the risks associated with not adapting to new conditions. Organizations will need to take on risk and explore change or have the market waves come figuratively crashing down upon their heads.

3. I NEEDED TO CHANGE

CHANGING LANDSCAPE

A changing landscape was on the horizon, and I realized that in my current situation, it was going to be hard for me to embrace the new conditions, adapt my skills, and feel confident in how I could take on and explore risk. At the time, my questions were, "How could I push for change within my organization and not be seen as someone trying to climb the ladder? How could I innovate within my organization when my company was struggling due to the extreme conditions outside the organization?" Coming up with answers to these questions was difficult, but with the landscape changing as fast as it was, I needed to develop a plan for adapting to the conditions so that I wasn't slammed by them. There was a sense of urgency, but also some caution, since I really wasn't sure what the conditions were like, what skills I would need, and how much risk I was willing to take on.

CHANGING SKILLS

After over fifteen years of professional work, I had built up and developed some sales and marketing skills as well as some good knowledge about the retail and healthcare industries. But I was at a crossroads. I knew I could build from that knowledge and those skills I had acquired, but I knew that in order to stay competitive and advance in my career, I was going to need to learn some new skills. I realized my mindset needed to change, and I needed to take a new approach to how I viewed my own skills and capabilities. I was going to need to abandon some of the skills that were no longer relevant or would hold me back from moving forward. And at the same time, I needed to build new skills that would meet the changes in the conditions that were happening around me. I would have to be more progressive in terms of how I thought about what I could do. I would also need to risk heading in a new direction in order to make this change happen.

CHANGE IN DIRECTION

After developing a plan, I decided to begin my new journey and step out into these new conditions. This change would help me adapt to what was happening in the market. I would learn new skills and capabilities, and I would take on more professional risk than I ever had before. I decided to put myself into harm's way whenever possible in order to move forward and willingly accept the new challenges regardless of the risk. The new direction would be a way for me to understand the new conditions, learn something new, and minimize the risk of making a major career change. In order to change, I needed this new direction. While I was uncertain about where

I was headed or what I was getting myself into, I knew that to change, I needed to do this.

WHAT I DID AND WHAT I LEARNED

1. THE SURF STORY AND THE WORK STORY

MALIBU

My journey in this new direction happened over the course of a few years. During this time, two key experiences shaped how I would answer my questions. These experiences would also provide a valuable lesson and a way for me to approach these kinds of challenges in the future. The first experience happened during a trip to Los Angeles, California and included my first attempt at ocean surfing in Malibu. It's hard to describe the pain, frustration, and utter failure I felt after my first ocean surfing experience. However, this failure would serve as the starting point for me to think about ways to help manage my professional career, and I would use the lessons from that day to take on even bigger challenges in the future. My first experience at Malibu was humbling, but it taught me about the power of the ocean as well as the principles of surfing, and it also gave me lessons to take into other areas of my life as well.

PRODUCT LAUNCH

In addition to experiencing the challenges of surfing, I had a few professional wipeouts that shaped my journey and influenced my decisions for how to manage my professional career. One of these experiences included a failed product launch and a challenging meeting with a top customer at the time. This was my first hint at what changes were to come and became a marker for when my journey really began. What I discovered was that I was not alone in my experiences, and that these changes were widespread—almost a universal sentiment that was reverberating through the business, specifically in marketing and sales. This situation was happening regardless of the industry, market, product, or service. Organizations were experiencing a massive shift in how they were marketing and selling products and services, but also in how they solved problems and met the increasing demands of customers in these new conditions.

FAILURE

Both the Surf Story and the Work Story had such similar elements and themes of failure that it was hard not to draw comparisons between them. Each experience offered optimistic expectations about the outcome, but also a discovery that the conditions or realities of the situation were much different than originally planned. In both situations, I discovered that I had a lack of skills in certain areas that I had not planned for and had not anticipated how challenging the conditions would be. Each story contained a certain amount of risk and a chance that the experience might not go as planned. When both stories are viewed in relation to one another, they take on a new dynamic than they would on their own and a new perspective of what went wrong and what I could have done differently.

2. SPORT AND WORK PARALLEL

CONDITIONS

In both the Surf Story and the Work Story, a parallel can be drawn to how the conditions in each of the respective areas were a major factor for determining someone's success. Within surfing, the conditions can dictate the success of catching a wave and can also determine whether or not you will walk away alive from the experience. The conditions within surfing are always changing, and surf reporting has made it easier to know whether or not there will be waves. But to truly understand the surf conditions, you need to be physically in the water. In the business world, the conditions can refer to the industry, the market, and also the conditions within an organization. Evaluating the market conditions is important, and there are numerous industry reports, blogs, and market research available to business leaders to gain new knowledge. But again, to know and understand what to do with that information, you need to be active in your market to know what's going on.

SKILLS

Surfers are constantly trying to improve their skills and abilities to get better at their sport. Surfing is the foundation for all boardsports—a group that also includes skateboarding and snowboarding. The word Progression is used to describe how someone is adding new skills as well as progressing in their sport. The idea of progression is foundational to boardsports and separates surfing from a lot of other recreational activities. The term progression has a lot of meaning for surfers, and it's more critical to the sport than it would be for others. For business professionals, we think about our skills as being acquired through years of experience and remaining relatively static until we decide to build new ones. Skills that belong to individuals can become organizational capabilities as long as the company retains those employees over time. Surfers tend to hold onto skills, build new ones, and then let them go. In the business world, we cling to our skills and let them define us as individuals and only seek out new ones when we must.

RISK

In addition to progressing, surfers are accustomed to risk within their sport, and there is a direct relationship to skills when it comes to exploring risk. The more risk a surfer takes on and explores, the more they can progress and improve. This is true for very few sports. Auto racing, skydiving, and few other sports have an inherent risk that can limit an individual's success within their sport. But surfing is a risk-driven sport with the surfer's ability to progress dependent on his or her willingness to explore risk. In the business world, we're exposed to risk but in a much different way. At times, risk may be financial; at other times, it may be professional. For the most part, however, unless you are a business owner, the amount of risk you are exposed to is actually very small. Most of us are not financially tied to our companies. We can make mistakes and still keep our jobs. And if things don't work out at one company, there's a good chance you can find a job at another.

3. WHAT I LEARNED

THE BRIDGE

The Surf Story and the Work Story were two separate yet challenging personal and professional situations. When the stories are looked at together with a bridge between them, a different perspective emerges. In both situations, I faced a set of new and challenging conditions that I had not experienced before. However, I realized that I had to develop some new skills and that I was resistant to this change and my tolerance for risk was also extremely low. I had some previous experience with boardsports but still failed to succeed at my first attempt at surfing. I knew that progression in my career would be a good thing, but I was not sure what next steps to take. I knew that I could not wait for the perfect conditions and that I had to change the way I was going to professionally surf these new conditions. My decision was either to get in the water or to stand on shore, watching the business world roll by me like a giant wave.

LATERALIZATION

In drawing a parallel between these two experiences, I came across a concept that helped me to bridge the two experiences and create a new view. The concept was *Lateralization* from the method of Lateral Thinking, developed by Edward de Bono. Dr. de Bono is a physician, psychologist, author, inventor, and consultant who originated the term "Lateral Thinking" to use as a technique to help people improve their thinking abilities and creativity skills. The concept is based on using a paradigm shift or an idea, framework, or model from one context in another. I asked myself, "How would a surfer approach these new business challenges? What would they do, even in the face of extreme risk?" To answer these questions, I adopted the mindset of the surfer, knowing that I would have "professional waves" crash down on my head and that I would have to paddle out into the "surf" again. Regardless of the conditions, my skills, or the risks involved, I had to do something different and take on new challenges if I was going to change.

THE NEW CHALLENGE

I decided to use what I learned from surfing in Malibu to change what I did professionally. My goal was to change how I approached my work and how I would look at my sales and marketing skills. The surfer would serve as the example to help me overcome these new challenges I was facing and to develop a process so that every time I experienced a new obstacle or challenge, I could find a way to be successful. As I started to work with this idea, I found that a set of principles existed that I could use as a repeatable process and that this process could help others overcome their own challenges as well. "Be More Like the Surfer" was the mantra stuck in my head. I used it over and over again to solve problems. I learned to use a set of three principles to stoke my professional career and ride the possibilities like a wave. This book will help you to use these principles to embrace new conditions, learn new skills, and take on risk so that you can ride the wave on your own.

THE PURPOSE OF THIS BOOK

1. MANAGE THE CHANGE

CUSTOMER BUYING POWER

This book will help business leaders embrace the change that's happening within markets, identify new skills to meet new customer demands, and develop a process to test or prototype new marketing and sales strategies. This book and process will also help organizations to manage this change and to understand the needs of their markets better. Customers are now able to leverage content from information-sharing platforms and make more informed buying decisions. They are also able to unbundle products and services to find better deals. Unbundling is a term used to describe how smaller organizations or start-ups are stripping services from larger, more established ones and offering those services in a more economical way. As technology continues to infiltrate markets and more established business models fall to the wayside, smaller and more nimble business models driven by technology will provide consumers with more information, more transparency, and more choice to make buying decisions.

NEW MINDSET

In order to manage this new change within markets, a new mindset will be needed as well—a mindset that is adaptable, can anticipate market shifts, and has the ability to change direction when markets become more challenging. The mindset of the past is based on traditional notions about how products are supposed to be marketed and sold. However, the current

RIDE THE WAVE

business environment has shown us that those long-held beliefs are outdated, or in some situations, completely false to begin with. The way to approach business now is with a progressive mindset focused on change, adaptability, and progressing professional skills to stay ahead in competitive markets. The new mindset is about skill-based progression and embracing these new changes consistently over time—not resting on previous success and fixed skills, but exploring new skills and evolving what you do to improve yourself and your organization.

EXPLORE CHANGE

"Ready, Aim, Fire" was the approach to change in the past. This thinking was how business leaders rolled out anything new and a way to protect themselves and the organization from risk. Now, it's the inverse. "Fire, Aim, Ready" is the approach for new conditions, pushing a new product or service into a market to test it, refine it, and make it better, working toward a "ready" position to expand and grow. Because changes are happening so rapidly, organizations will need to test and prototype products, ideas, and tactics to stay competitive. Design Thinking has become the standard for product design and development, but this approach has also made its way into other areas of business, including sales and marketing. A design-thinking process will need to be used to test ideas and strategies before they go to market. The surfer uses a similar process to build skills, and you will need to do the same in order to bring new products and services to customers.

2. THE PROCESS

EXTERNAL

Rigid internal processes, old mindsets, and the fear of failure have hamstrung organizations, forcing them to compete in fast-paced markets with outdated skills and mindsets that were impactful decades ago. If companies don't change and embrace the new conditions, the livelihood of the organization and the professional will continue to be exposed to these ever-changing conditions. This book provides examples to highlight the changes that are impacting markets and how business leaders can evaluate what's happening outside their organization. Just as a surfer evaluates the conditions before heading out into the water, sales and marketing leadership will need to constantly examine the conditions before doing anything new. Most organizations first look internally at systems, processes, and people before they consider the external market. They focus on the organization instead of considering what might be changing for their customers. The first step in the Ride the Wave Process is to look outside the organization and into the market conditions, evaluating what has changed, what is new, and what the organization will need to do differently because of these factors.

INTERNAL

Evaluating the external conditions will help you to understand the current market and your organization's place within it. An assessment of the internal skills and capabilities is also necessary to see how your capabilities inside the organization match the new external conditions. Just as a surfer knows the types of skills he or she has and what is possible on a wave, the business leader should know how his or her organizational capabilities align with the market or if a gap needs to be closed. The Ride the Wave Process helps you to think about your capabilities in terms of progression as well as to anticipate what will be needed next. With the goal of building organizational capabilities that are able to ride the waves of change and not put you back on the shore, this process provides an internal assessment and will help you to match the skills of your teams with what is happening in the market.

RISK

The external and internal views will provide you with the insight to begin the process of planning your next steps and the actions to be taken. This is not the traditional approach to strategy and setting a comfortable vision for the future, but more about preparing yourself to take on new risk in the short term. For surfers, risk is self-limiting. It's the main factor that will determine your level of success and if you are able to add new skills and capabilities. As a surfer, if you don't explore risk, you will not progress within your sport. Within the new conditions that we are experiencing within markets, the same is true for business leadership. If you aren't willing to explore new strategies or risk, someone else out there likely will. The organizations that are more aggressive, more skilled, and more willing to take on risk will survive and thrive in the new conditions.

3. RIDE THE WAVE

EMBRACE THE CONDITIONS

This book will walk you through the three main challenges we are all facing right now in business and provide you with a process to ride the market waves on your own. After reading this book, you'll have a better understanding of why markets have changed and what you can do about it in order to be successful. Embracing the conditions or managing the market is the first step to riding the wave. This is not reacting to market changes and being able to match what competition is doing. The process will help you create opportunities that will identify untapped market opportunities so you can lead in markets instead of follow. The process is universal and can be replicated across any industry or market. Regardless of your product or service, you'll be able to embrace the conditions and *ride the wave*.

CHANGE YOUR MINDSET

After reading this book and going through the process, you will have a new mindset. You will think differently about your current skills and the new skills you will need to acquire. New skills will seem less mystical, and the journey to acquiring them will be less daunting. This new mindset is built on progression and adding new skills and capabilities over time. It's not a winner-takes-all approach to skills where you either add them or you don't, but more about progressively adding skills to move you forward. We cram for tests and we binge exercise to lose weight, but we end up putting the weight back on because the new habits don't stick and we receive poor results from not studying more often. We all want everything in an instant with no effort or investment. When it doesn't work out, we assume it wasn't meant to be, or we ignore or dismiss the goal as not worth pursuing anymore. Instead, the new mindset will help you to understand your gaps and slowly build these new skills over time, and you will remain focused on the journey and progression.

EXPLORE RISK

When you decide to *ride the wave*, the results will bring more clarity around your market and skills. You will feel more confident with your approach to taking on and exploring risk. Risk exploration is the key to the process and riding the wave. Just as surfers need risk to progress in their sport, you will need to take on risk and will be tested again and again before you find success. Employment was once safe, and someone could work the same job for fifty years with little to no disruption to his or her career. In this new market, the average tenure for a marketing manager is forty-four months. The risks associated with employment are now a reality that we must all face. Long-term security from a career and financial incentives that went along with staying with a single employer are gone. The new conditions demand skills that are aligned with new market and new customer demands. As individuals, we must now see risk as part of the new conditions whether we like it or not. Anticipating changes in the market, adding new skills and capabilities, and exploring risk will be the new process for success.

SURF STORY: PART I

2

THE DREAM

1. OCEAN SURFING

THE MIDWEST

The first experience I had that led me to take this new professional journey started in the Midwest in the Land of 10,000 Lakes, far from the beaches and salt water of the Pacific Ocean. Growing up, the first sport I played was soccer. I also played in college as an NCAA Division III athlete. In high school, I was one of the best players on my team, but in college, I wasn't even the best guy in my dorm. Luckily, I had stayed engaged with boardsports such as skateboarding, snowboarding, and wakeboarding over the years and continued to participate in those sports as an adult. Boardsports were a hobby and something I could do 100 percent on my own. Unlike soccer, which is a heavy team sport, boardsports gave me an outlet to do something as an individual, and the time I have spent off the soccer pitch has been spent doing boardsports.

CALIFORNIA DREAMING

Because I spent so much time participating in boardsports over the years, I learned about the history and significance that each of them has to the sport of surfing. Surfing is the foundational sport for all other boardsports. It's one of the most progressive action sports and has continued to stay relevant over the years when so many mainstream sports have seen their participation levels fade. Being from the Midwest, surfing was a dream. Since I hadn't spent much time in or around the ocean, the sport seemed out of reach, something that only came with coastal living. I was always attracted to the sport because it was so different from anything I had done in sports before. I dreamed about what it would be like to be in the ocean among the waves. Given that I had participated in other boardsports for years, surfing seemed like something I might be able to do. I wanted to cross it off my boardsports bucket list.

THE DREAM

As I began to think more and more about my surfing dream, I convinced myself that ocean surfing was something that I could do. I was driven to make this dream a reality, and I started to think more about how I could make it happen. I just needed to go to an ocean. While planning for this adventure, I would stumble across online ads for a surf trip to Costa Rica. Or I would see videos online of surfers riding massive waves in Hawaii, Australia, and South Africa. As I started to solidify my plans, I realized that a surfing trip would be as easy as jumping on a flight and heading to the west coast. I began to put my ideas to paper and started to map out my surf adventure. And without knowing it at the time, this simple decision would serve as the inspiration for a major career change and also the genesis for this book.

2. PREPARATION

JAWS

As I began to put together the plan that would launch my surf adventure, it became clear that my knowledge about the sport was very limited. I had spent some time wakesurfing behind a boat and was pretty good at riding waves. But that was in a freshwater lake that had little to no real risks other than the occasional boat or rogue jet skier. Up until I decided to try ocean surfing, my primary point of reference for the ocean was the movie *Jaws*. I was terrified of the ocean and even more terrified of sharks. I did realize that I would actually have a better chance of being struck by lightning, killed in a car accident, or dying from a fireworks accident. But as irrational as these thoughts were about the ocean, I was still terrified to go into the water and scared to death about what might be lurking below the surface.

SURF BREAKS

Knowing that I would need to overcome my fear of sharks and brave the ocean, I created a map of all the surf spots in and around the greater Los Angeles area. I had been to LA before and knew the city, so I was comfortable going back and spending a few days surfing. The coast of California from the north to the south offers numerous spots, almost too many to choose from, and the list was not only impressive but incredibly intimidating. El Porto, Hermosa Beach, Manhattan Beach, Venice Beach, and Surfrider Beach in Malibu were on a list of some of the best surf spots in the world. I decided that Surfrider Beach would be an ideal spot since it has a long and slow break that easily covers the length of three football fields and would be an ideal spot for someone trying ocean surfing for the first time. The break occupied the space between

Malibu Lagoon and Malibu Pier. It was gorgeous. It was clean and accessible. And for someone from the Midwest, it looked liked paradise.

LOGISTICS

As I mapped out the plan, my confidence started to grow. I had planned every step I would take, from jumping on the plane in Minneapolis to planting my feet on the beach in Malibu. I picked a day during our trip that my girlfriend, Kate, and I would surf by looking at the surfline.com report. There is an HD camera at Malibu that allows you to see the current conditions, and from the live video feed, I saw that there were waves. For my plan, I also figured out the best route from the hotel to Malibu Beach and knew that the Malibu Surf Shack was 367 feet from Surfrider Beach. I could easily walk from the rental shop with my board, wetsuit, and boots. And based on my plan, I knew that if I went on a weekday, there would be fewer people and that I had a better chance of having the waves all to myself.

3. PLANNING

The Plan

After four weeks of meticulously mapping out every step of this adventure, I had a dozen printed pages of planning materials in a Word document and had acquired more information about surfing than I could have ever possibly imagined. I had spent my free nights putting together what I thought was a rock-solid plan. In my professional life, I was known as a planner. I would build sales and marketing plans by analyzing data, developing tactics, and creating action plans. In my mind, this was going to be no different than anything I had done previously in my professional career. I had been successful for years working under the assumption that as long as I had a good plan, I was going to be successful. Even though this plan was for surfing and not for business, I thought I could fall back on my previous boardsports experience and use my planning skills to make this happen.

ON PAPER

On paper, there was no doubt in my mind that I was going to surf. I had done my homework and put together a good plan. I had also spent over twenty years skateboarding, snowboarding, or wakeboarding. I knew that if it was a flat board with grip tape, bindings, or boots, there was a good chance I could ride it. I knew that with my plan, I had done what I needed to do in order to put myself in a position to surf. But I also wanted to talk to surfers who had done this before. After my plan was completed, I talked to other surfers to gain insight from those that had done this before and knew what to expect. I was able to ask questions, get some tips, and solidify my planning even more. My paper plan started to come to life with the input from actual surfers and, mentally, I felt like I was moving closer to making my dreams a reality.

IN MY MIND

As I continued to reach out to other surfers that had actually spent time in the water, I gathered additional information, garnered support, and received instructions on what I needed to do. I did receive new information during this process, but a lot of what I was told simply verified everything I had put together in my plan. People are naturally optimistic and want to help others succeed, so during my conversations, I was told that this would be "no big deal" and that with my experience in boardsports, surfing would be easy and just like snowboarding or wakeboarding. The more I talked to people who had surfed, the more confident I felt that this was going to happen. I was imagining the best possible outcome and had a new sense of confidence from my planning. I had done my homework and asked all the right questions. Now, all that was left was to jump on a plane and fly 1,900 miles across the country to the Pacific Ocean.

THE REALITY

1. MALIBU

WAKE-UP CALL

After Kate and I spent the first part of our trip taking in the sights and sounds of LA, I was ready to surf. I had enjoyed my time leading up to our Malibu adventure, but somehow, the first part of the trip felt like a distraction from the true intention of our visit to the west coast. So much work and effort had gone into the planning and preparation for the surfing that I basically sleepwalked through the days leading up to what was going to be the main event. The day of, Kate and I woke up to our alarm at 5:00 a.m., had breakfast, and hit the road before most of California had gotten out of bed that morning. We had the road to ourselves and would eventually have the beach to ourselves that day as well. In choosing a weekday, we knew that there would be no crowds and fewer surfers in the water. I wanted the waves to myself and didn't want to compete for spots in a lineup. Going early made sense and was all part of the plan.

PCH 1

Malibu was only a thirty-minute drive from our hotel in Santa Monica up the Pacific Coast Highway, but the short trip seemed to take hours. As we got closer to Malibu, we hit a bit of traffic and a few stoplights along the way. Each stop increased the sense of anticipation and made us more and more anxious the closer we got to our destination. I was nervous about the surfing and all the unknowns awaiting me in the ocean. Kate did not know what to expect and had not been a part of my planning, so we exchanged nervous banter about the traffic, pointed out the beautiful houses along the way, and enthusiastically scanned the ocean through the car windows, looking for waves. My hands were locked in a "10 and 2" death grip on the steering wheel. I felt like I was already holding on for dear life. I pulled my hands off the wheel once in a while and held them in front of the air conditioning vents to cool them down before placing them back on the wheel. As we got closer to Malibu, we started to notice boards strapped to the roofs of cars, crammed into backseats, or sticking out of windows. We were getting close.

THE SURF SHACK

We arrived in Malibu and found a place to park for the day before starting our short walk to the Surf Shack. Kate and I continued with our nervous banter, talking each other into what we were about to do. We rented boards from two guys at the Malibu Surf Shack. They were the two most relaxed people I had ever met in my life, and they were very nonchalant about the whole experience. I rented a surfboard, a wetsuit, and a pair of boots. One of the guys who helped us (who had longer hair than Kate and no shirt on) helped me with my board. His response to my questions about the surf and a passing question about local shark activity was basically to scoff, and he all but dismissed them. His extreme confidence made me think my concerns were hysterics and that I would be fine. I reminded myself that I had put together a masterful plan and that he was right. I would be fine.

2. THE CONDITIONS

MOMENT OF ZEN

We made the short walk down to the beach, and what I saw was everything I could have hoped for and more. Crystal sand, bright blue water, clear skies, and waves breaking not too far from shore. I started to put on my wetsuit and boots. My mind was racing, and I started to feel a wave of adrenaline from the realization that I had finally reached my destination. Kate helped me gather my clothes and our valuables and also to formulate my plan to enter the water. When I was ready to go, I stood on the beach, looked out across the water, and thought, "Let's do this." The first part of my planning was accomplished. I put in the work. Made it to the beach. Now it was time to surf. As I started to walk down the beach toward the water, I swore I could hear the Beach Boys singing "Good Vibrations" in the background, with the theremin calling out to me from the water. Feeling a final moment of zen, I took a deep breath and walked out into the water.

OCEAN CHALLENGES

As I got deeper into the water, I noticed the rocks under my feet. They were slippery, round, and very large. As my feet slid off the rocks and got wedged into the cracks between them, I thought to myself, "Good thing I have these boots on or this would be brutal." The further I got out into the water, the more difficult it was to walk. I was slipping on rocks, the water was getting deeper, and the waves started to push me back toward the shore. Deciding that my feet had taken enough abuse, I made an attempt to jump on my board and tried to paddle the rest of the way. But as waves crashed onto the shore and receded back into the water, it became pretty awkward, since I was only in about eighteen inches of water. I was literally lying on my board, pulling myself over large rocks. I also encountered large beds of kelp that had pooled and collected just off the shoreline. I paddled through the kelp, which was disgusting, and ended up having it caught in my ankle strap, dragging the kelp beds with me as I made my way away from shore.

THE PACIFIC

As I got farther out into the water, I was able to shake the kelp loose, but then encountered small sets of waves that were now rolling in toward shore. The waves got increasingly larger the farther I went out, and it got to the point where they were starting to break. I knew that I would need to dive under these waves in order to move past them and find a calm place in the lineup just past the impact area. I began to "duck dive" under the waves, but kept being pushed back in the direction I was coming from, taking a mouthful of salt water each time and frantically paddling through each incoming wave. Having made it through a few sets of waves, I reached the lineup where I could stop and regroup. I was happy to have made it this far, but unfortunately, I was physically drained from having to paddle through an oceanic gauntlet of obstacles. Any energy I did have was gone. I had not surfed a single wave, and yet I was dead tired, having just experienced one of the most powerful forces in nature. The Pacific Ocean.

3. SKILL GAPS

INSTANT FATIGUE

After making it to the lineup about 100 yards offshore, I was instantly fatigued. I had paddled only a short distance, but I quickly realized that I had no upper body strength or arm or shoulder strength, and that all the weightlifting I had done over the years was absolutely useless in the ocean. New muscles, or muscles I didn't know I had, were on fire, literally burning under my wetsuit. Even as I began to paddle myself into the lineup, I could tell that my arms weren't going to last much longer and that I would need to take breaks in order to just attempt to paddle toward an incoming wave. Having planned this trip for weeks in advance, I can honestly say that I never even considered the physical aspects of surfing and just figured I would have the strength and ability once I got into the water. However, the longer I stayed in the water, the more my gaps started to appear and the more I could start seeing the first set of flaws in my planning.

AIR IS GOOD

In addition to my lack of physical strength, I started to notice my breathing was very heavy. Not only was I exerting a lot of physical effort and using large amounts of oxygen to paddle through the water, but I also had to hold my breath every few minutes to duck under an approaching wave. After a few minutes of this, I realized that not only was I a poor swimmer, but I couldn't hold my breath for more than a few seconds without having to get to the surface for some air. With all the physical effort I was putting into paddling and holding my breath to avoid waves, I realized that I hadn't really planned for this much swimming and never thought that my cardio would be taking such a toll. I was also a runner and had been training for races at the time. I was in decent shape, but this was far different from running and something I had never experienced before in all my years swimming in lakes and pools. It was one of the first times in my life when drowning became a real possibility.

SURF OR SURVIVE

As I started to settle myself on my board and was finally able to catch my breath, I started to think less about survival and more about surfing. My adrenaline started to kick in, and I said to myself, "You flew all the way out here, so it's time to catch some waves." As I paddled toward the lineup, I could see the water swell and rise just in front of me on the horizon. It was crazy to see the water pitch up and a wave build from what seemed like nowhere. As I saw waves break, I would have to turn on my board in the water, reposition myself to face the shore, and then start to paddle like a maniac in order to match the speed of the waves. With almost no energy left and no experience timing the breaking waves, I ended up being either too far back and behind where the waves were breaking or out in front of the wave and had it break or crash down on top of my head. After two or three failed attempts and a couple of close calls, it was back to survival mode.

SLAMMED ON THE BEACH

1. "GET BACK ON THE BEACH"

LOCALS RULE

In between catching my breath and trying to avoid increasingly larger waves, I noticed the reactions of the other surfers around me. It was fairly obvious at that point to everyone in the water who the local surfers were and who the kook from out of town was. Knowing about localism and the unwritten rules about surf spots from watching Keanu Reeves in *Point Break*, I knew that these waves did not belong to me, and I was just a guest in the surfers' water. I tried as much as possible to be accommodating and only took opportunities on waves that other surfers were not pursuing. Meaning, I basically got the scraps. I got what was left over and spent more time moving out of people's way and less time actually surfing. But the longer I was out there, the more comfortable I became. I started to make small talk and even make some small allegiances with the surfers that were sympathetic to my cause. As I started to feel more confident, I relaxed and was able to regain some energy that I had lost during the first part of my session.

WAVE SETS

There was a brief lull in the number of waves coming in—until a surfer farther up shore yelled out "Outside!" to the group and then turned to paddle out into deeper water. Just over his shoulder, I could see the water start to pitch up just like before, but this time, the water started to rise up at a faster pace, and the horizon started to disappear completely. As the wave broke, I could see white water form on the top of the wave, and the sound of rushing water became louder and louder as it roared toward me. As the wave started to barrel, surfers were paddling ferociously either to catch the wave or to paddle out of the way. This massive wave rolled by me, and I did everything I could to avoid getting pummeled by it or run over by a surfer on it. Having survived for the moment, I looked back to see another wave that was bigger than the first coming right toward me. Everyone in the water at the time had either caught the wave or got out of its way. Unfortunately for me, I was in the wrong place at the wrong time and got caught "inside" the impact zone.

TOMBSTONING

A massive wave picked me up and slammed me down on the water like a WWE wrestler would body slam his opponent down onto a mat. I was pushed under the water upside down, and it was so dark that I couldn't tell the surface of the water from the bottom of the ocean. My board was attached to my ankle by a leash, and it started doing something called "tombstoning," where you are pulled so far down under the water that the leash pulls the board from the back end and makes the board stick out of the water like a tombstone in a cemetery. I reached up, grabbed the leash at my ankle, and literally started to pull myself up to the surface. Knowing that this was my only lifeline to safety. Reaching the surface, I started to gasp for air. For my sake, a local surfer grabbed me by the back of my wetsuit and gave me a very direct piece of advice. "Hey dude, you have no business being out here. Get your ass back on the shore."

2. SLAMMED ON THE BEACH

BACK ON THE BEACH

After getting scolded by one of the local surfers and finally making it back onto my board, I did a combination of dog-paddling and bodysurfing back to shore. The water started to empty from my lungs, and my eyes, now burning from the salt water, started to readjust to the sunlight. I could now make out Kate standing on the shore, watching me. As I got closer to shore, I had to reverse navigate the gauntlet course of kelp beds, stumble over the slippery rocks, and then try to walk up the shore with what dignity I had left. I was exhausted, and every muscle in my body was aching. I dropped my board on the beach and stood in silence for a few minutes next to Kate. With water still dripping everywhere, and my legs shaking with fatigue, I started to pull off my wetsuit. I asked Kate, "So, how bad was that?"

Her response: "Well, the lifeguard got out of her chair and was standing on the shore watching you, so yeah. It was pretty bad."

"Great," I said. "That's great. I'm happy to have given her something to do this morning."

TIME-OUT

After one of the most harrowing experiences of my life, it was time to press pause, take a time-out, and regroup a bit. I parked my butt on the beach, grabbed a towel, and started to think about what just went down. In reflecting on what happened, I had a weird feeling of shock and disbelief. Considering how much time and effort I had put into the planning for this trip, it was hard to understand where it went wrong. But at the same time, I felt an honest recognition and acceptance of the fact that I was not as thought-out or prepared as I should have been. This was somehow a feeling of shock, and it also made perfect sense at the same time. Even though it was just a few minutes after this near disaster, I could again see the flaws in my planning. As I started to relive the challenges I encountered in my head, it was painfully obvious where this plan went wrong and where mistakes were made. I took a few more minutes to regroup physically, but also to reflect mentally a little bit more on what had just happened.

TIME TO REGROUP

Sitting on the beach at Malibu, thinking about what had happened, I walked back through the morning in an attempt to figure out how or where I went wrong. Coming into the trip, I had spent so much time and effort on the plan that I thought little about what it would actually take to surf and what I needed to expect once I got into the conditions. Planning the first part of the adventure had gone so smoothly that it just seemed natural that the success would continue during the actual surfing and that I would easily accomplish what I had set out to do. But having just experienced the raw power of Mother Nature and the challenges of the ocean firsthand, I realized I had to figure out what I had missed during my planning and why my plan didn't translate into reality. The ocean conditions were something I had not experienced before, and I realized the assumptions I made were untested and that this was the first place I went astray in my planning.

3. "WHAT JUST HAPPENED?"

THE CONDITIONS

As Kate and I sat on the beach in Malibu, I thought long and hard about the reasons why I had failed. I thought about the reality of the actual surf conditions and how most of my plan was built around the logistics of the trip and how I would travel to the ocean. I gave little thought to what actual challenges I would face once I was in the water. Even though I had the right equipment, I didn't anticipate the rocks, kelp beds, and the power of the waves. I had not anticipated aspects of the conditions, and the realities of the conditions were far more challenging than what I had planned for. It was not until I actually walked into the water and started to paddle out that I understood what those conditions were like. You could read about surfing in a book or online but still not fully understand or appreciate the conditions until you put yourself in them.

MY SKILLS

Physically, all I could feel was pain throughout my entire body. The bottoms of my feet were stinging from the rocks, every muscle was aching, and my lungs burned from the salt water and a temporary lack of oxygen. I had spent the weeks leading up to this trip doing my regular workout routine and staying in relatively good shape. I just assumed that one type of physical fitness would translate to another and that would be okay. I was sure my current physical strength would help me through the experience and that my history with boardsports would make this just another day on a board for me. I did not know how tough it would be, how poorly my body was conditioned for surfing, or that I didn't have the right skills for the sport. The gap between where I was with my surfing skills and where I needed to be was a massive gap that now seemed almost impossible to close.

THE RISKS

After thinking about the conditions and the skills I lacked for surfing, I also started to reflect on how much of a risk I just took. Again, this was something I didn't even consider in my planning. The risk of drowning was something I had not planned for but was now a very real possibility. Without the assistance of one of my fellow surfers and under different circumstances, this could have been far worse. In all my weeks of planning leading up to this day, I didn't even think about the possibility of injuries. I didn't think about failure, and I didn't plan for it. Thankfully, I had Kate there to remind me over lunch, then over dinner, and then again before bedtime, how I almost drowned in the ocean. The more we talked about it and laughed, the more we started to see some of the humor in it and how crazy it was for me to actually give surfing a shot. Unfortunately, this experience with planning and failure wouldn't be my last, but instead something I would experience again in the near future.

WORK STORY: PART I 3

THE DREAM

1. BLOCKBUSTER SALES

THE EXPERT

Around the same time I ventured out to Malibu and almost drowned in the Pacific Ocean, I was well into my career at a healthcare company where I had worked for the previous ten years. I had held a few different roles at that point, supported company-wide sales and marketing projects, and completed my MBA. I did well in my roles because I was organized, I stuck to the plan, and my customers seemed to respond well to the way we marketed and sold our products. My customers saw me as a resource and an expert when it came to how our products could help patients. We had products that were market leaders, I was trained well, and I was passionate about my job. For almost a decade, I had experienced some level of success and thought that success would always continue without stopping anytime soon.

SALES AND MARKETING

A strong marketing and sales organization, our company

used a strategy that was always the same. Marketing would put together the plan and sales would execute. Our sales force was considered one of the best in the industry, and we had achieved "blockbuster status" with two products that were considered the gold standard treatments within their healthcare specialty. We had executed the same game plan for years and experienced a lot of great success. As an organization, we focused on "working the plan" because that's what worked. If someone was struggling and not making their numbers, we would say, "Stick to the plan." This internal mantra guided the organization, and we made a name for ourselves by doing things that way. When we rolled out any new sales or marketing initiative, we would also customize that plan for our customers based on the market they were in, since certain parts of the country had different barriers or obstacles to our products. There were subtleties with coverage and even with the way customers interacted with the sales organization. Understanding the new initiative was always important, but then you had to figure out how best to execute that plan in the field.

PREPARATION AND PLANNING

Shortly after my trip to Malibu, our organization was in the process of launching a new product within our specialty niche, and we were bringing a new product to a market in which we had a strong share. This new product would not be another blockbuster but would be a nice addition to our portfolio and would solve a need for patients that was not currently being met in the market. In order to prepare and be ready for the product launch, we went through the same process we always did. Even though we were the market leaders, respected by our customers, we still needed to make sure we executed our plans properly and brought the same level of expertise to this product launch that we had brought in the past. During the weeks leading up to our launch date, I started training on the new product, learning the technical aspects of how it worked, and most importantly, the new benefits to our patients.

2. TRAINING DAY

HOME AND FIELD TRAINING

There were two parts to the training for a new product launch: at-home training and in-the-field training. There would also be training at the official launch meeting in the coming weeks. The launch meeting was essentially a national sales and marketing meeting attended by almost everyone from within the organization. We had to study at night and were tasked with completing training assignments during the day while still in the field. Training was in addition to managing a territory, completing project work, and meeting with customers. Regardless of the upcoming launch, it was business as usual for the organization. The expectation was that business did not drop off because of the launch and that regular day-to-day activities were still completed. This situation was challenging, considering that training included learning the marketing plan, the messaging and positioning, the entire package insert, and a series of tests to develop your ability to quickly recall the information.

SALES AND MARKETING PLAN

We were launching a new type of product, but within an established and well-defined market. Our product would solve an unmet need, and from the market research we had done, our customers were very receptive to the new opportunity to treat this type of patient. What we assumed about the market was that we could launch under our new indication and then add additional indications as the market started to become more comfortable with our product. On paper, this was the right strategy and the best way to approach the product launch. This approach made a lot of sense from the standpoint of our launch strategy, but it really gave our customers the opportunity to progress through a treatment method and expand their product usage over time. It also made sense from the standpoint of offering a new product with a specific indication so that we did not cannibalize our current book of business with a product that was new to the market. Again, on paper, the plan was solid, and the expectation was that this launch would be another success.

PLANNING TO LAUNCH

Prior to the launch meeting, I had set up meetings with the key customers in my territory. I wanted to return from the launch meeting and hit the ground running. To do that, I set daily appointments for the first four weeks coming out of our launch meeting. I wanted my workdays to be productive, and putting meetings on the calendar in advance would allow me to focus on selling versus prospecting or appointment setting. I wanted to wake up every morning, jump in my car, and go "chop wood" in my territory. I knew that the faster I got my customers up and running with the new product, the better my results would be. I anchored my days with morning appointments where I would bring breakfast into offices, had lunch meetings with preordered food from the day before, and filled the midmorning and mid to late afternoon timeslots with shorter meetings that were made based on territory routing and drop-in calls. During the four weeks leading up to launch, I had my schedule wire-tight and was ready to go.

3. LAUNCH MEETING

MEETING EVENTS

After four weeks of completing online tests and spending every free minute I had learning the new product, I was ready to attend the launch meeting. Once there, the pace didn't slow down at all. It intensified. We watched presentations from marketing, sales, operations, and our leadership teams. It was impressive. Each functional area had a motivating message, was focused on the product strategy, and gave us the tools we needed to be successful in the field. It was amazing to see the entire organization focused and so well prepared for the task at hand. The goal was having a successful launch, but helping customers and patients in the process. This week was filled with more tests and certifications, the dreaded role-play, and evening events that were more like rock concerts than business meetings. A lot of learning took place, but more importantly, there was an effort to bring the marketing and sales teams together and have everyone fired up for the challenges ahead.

CONFIDENT COWORKERS

After a full week of intense training, I was ready. I talked to my coworkers, and they were ready too. We talked about our customers and which ones would start using the new product right away, but also about the benefits that came along with the new product for patients. Admittedly, we also talked about the financial incentives that would be tied to our eventual successes and what we would do with the rewards that went along with success. Coming out of the meeting, I was energized, focused, and believed firmly in what we had learned over the previous weeks. For the organization, this was business as usual. We had been in this position before, having launched successful products previously. We had gone through training like this in the past, and we knew how to execute in the field. We could implement on marketing and sales plans better than anyone else in our particular industry. We were beyond confident and ready to go.

MY KOL

Coming out of the launch meetings, I began to think about the KOL I had in my territory. A Key Opinion Leader is someone who the organization deems as having a tremendous amount of knowledge about the disease state and experience in the best products to treat patients. I had an appointment with the top KOL in my territory the first day of the field launch. He was one of the highest prescribers in the state and ranked nationally for the number of patients he treated. I knew that having this customer up and running with our new product would make or break my launch. It was important that I met with him right away to make sure he had all the information he needed to use our product. I had a great relationship with this customer and felt confident in the fact that I had just gone through my training and knew that our plan along with my experience would be a recipe for success.

THE REALITY

1. DON'T TEACH ME

KOL LUNCH

On the first day out of the launch meeting, I had so much anticipation for the day ahead. I was brimming with confidence, having just returned from training, and felt great about having scheduled a meeting with my KOL. I put on my favorite suit, had a big breakfast, and gave Kate a kiss as I went out the door. That morning I made a few calls to get my feet wet with the new sales message, but I knew that my big moment was coming up later that day and that my KOL lunch would put my entire launch into motion. In preparing for the lunch meeting, I had preordered the customer his favorite meal—a meatball sandwich, BBQ chips, and Orange Fanta. The sandwich shop did not have Orange Fanta, so I had to make a couple additional stops, but finally found Fanta at a gas station not far from the customer's office. I spent a few minutes putting together marketing packets of information for the customer and the rest of the staff as well as reviewing the launch materials before the meeting. During my pre-call planning, I reviewed the sales data for the customer, wrote out some notes, and planned what I would say during the call. I was ready to go.

PERSONAL RELATIONSHIP

In terms of my relationships with customers, the one I had with this KOL was by far the best I had with any of my customers over the ten-year period. Having called on this provider for years, I knew his favorite movies, that his kids went to the same school where I did my undergraduate work, and that he saw me as an expert in terms of what I knew about his patients and practice. My call strategy was to go through our product information, and in the end, get him to agree with what I was saying about our new product and how the benefits would be a breakthrough for his untreated patients. Coming out of the launch meeting and feeling confident, my plan was to continue to play the role of the expert, and I was going to go through the information as I had done during my training. It was time to leverage that great relationship I had with him and jump-start this launch.

THE CALL

After making some small talk on the front end of the call, I waited for the rest of the staff to leave the lunch area. As my KOL started to take the first bite of his meatball sandwich, I decided it was time to start my call. As the sandwich moved toward his mouth for the first bite, I grabbed my presentation and launched into the call. As I started to go through the front cover, focusing on the message and positioning our product, I noticed a change in the energy within the room. The meatball sandwich dropped onto his plate and a hand stretched out toward me as if it were happening in slow motion. He slapped the presentation piece down and onto the table. Shock waves went through my body as I reeled back from what had just happened. Not knowing what just happened, I looked up and made direct eye contact with my customer, who looked me dead in the eyes and said, "Don't you try and teach me about your product."

2. NEW DECISION JOURNEY

EXPERT CUSTOMERS

In the decade of calls prior to this one, this had never happened before. Not knowing how to react, since my customers typically saw me as the expert, I was so taken aback by what happened that I paused and asked politely, "Excuse me?" There was a deafening silence in the room and a long pause from my customer. "Don't. Don't try and teach me about this product." Still back-pedaling and trying to figure out what had just happened, I honored the customer's request. Instead of going through the presentation I had just spent the last four weeks learning, I started to ask some questions and then listened for a long time. As the customer started to describe what he had been doing during the four weeks I was at training, I was shocked to hear how much he knew about our product, what he did to educate himself, and how I just lost control of a sales call that I had been planning for weeks in advance.

NEW CONDITIONS

For years, my customers had seen me as the expert. Yet, somehow this customer knew everything about my product, including how and where to use it. He had come to these conclusions independent of meeting with me and done this on his own. In the four weeks leading up to our meeting, he had visited a microsite to learn more about the product. This customer had participated in a webinar and learned about the product from his colleagues. He had visited patient-driven websites that discussed the product, its potential adverse events, and how patients could benefit from a trial. And most surprisingly, he had already started to use the product, identifying patient profiles within his practice and using the product as he saw fit. In four weeks, he had found all the information he needed, gone through a decision journey on his own, and had already made up his mind about how and where he was going to use our product. In that moment, I realized that everything I thought I knew about sales and marketing had changed.

THE CHANGE

My role had changed. I was no longer the expert. My customer was now an expert too. With all the information that was available, this customer had circumvented our marketing-to-sales process and become an expert on his own. I had prepared for weeks, going through the materials and learning about the product. This customer had done the exact same thing, just without my help or support. This was tough to take at first, but I quickly realized that my role of expert had changed and that if he had come to new conclusions about our product on his own, then I needed to find out what those were, so that I could best support him and his practice. Instead of going through my presentation, I found out where he planned to use our product and if those plans were different from what my organization and I had planned. This customer had done his own research, made up his mind, and knew everything he wanted to know about our product. The problem was that it was very different from what we had planned for and not at all close to what we put down on paper.

3. NEW WAY TO BUY

NEW CUSTOMER DECISION JOURNEY

I did what I could to salvage the call, but I definitely felt the sting of being professionally punched in the face by one of my customers. My KOL and I left things on good terms, but there was a noticeable change in our interactions from that day forward. What happened on that call was not just specific to this particular customer. As I continued to make additional calls, I noticed that something similar was happening across my territory. Customers already knew the material I was presenting and had come to a conclusion about how they planned to use our product before I could meet with them. The customer went through a new decision journey that I had not expected and that my company had not planned for. Our customers had leveraged the new technology that was available in healthcare, had spent their own time doing research, and moved through a buying process without the help of anyone from the sales organization. They became self-informed and walked themselves through a new decision journey completely independent of anyone from our organization.

NEW SKILLS AND CAPABILITIES

As a result of what was happening to myself and others in the field, my company had to change the way we were going to approach this launch. The company held conference calls and meetings to discuss what was happening. It had become obvious that situations like the one I had experienced were happening across the country and that these were not isolated incidents. Our customers now had a new way to buy, and we now had to change our approach, adapt to the market, and learn some new skills in the process. So much of our training up to that point had been focused on product knowledge and understanding how the medication would benefit a specific set of patients that we failed to plan for our customers becoming educated on the product and deciding on their own where and how they would use it.

NEW APPROACH TO RISK

Instead of falling back on strategies and tactics that had worked for us in the past, we had to start doing things that were new. We had to take a different approach and try to meet our customers where they were along this new decision journey. We had to try things that were new and that were going to be a risk. We needed to hit certain goals and metrics during the launch, and at the rate we were going, it was obvious we would not hit those projections. New sets of skills brought new training, and it was even more challenging to have everyone across the organization on the same page. It was tough to change as an individual and even tougher to change the internal processes and systems from the way we had done things in the past. This would take time, cause more headaches, and slow down our launch momentum, even before we had a chance to get it off the ground. From this point forward, things were different. Before long, serious change started to happen industry-wide, and it was obvious that we were not the only ones experiencing titanic shifts in the market conditions.

SLAMMED IN THE OFFICE

1. "WHAT JUST HAPPENED"

INDUSTRY CHANGES

Much like my experience in Malibu, I was left professionally "slammed" in an office. I had been crushed by the new way customers were buying, and my organization was being pounded by wave after wave of change within these new conditions. This had become another moment where I was thinking to myself, "What just happened?" I had spent weeks planning for this launch, but somehow, I got wiped out by market changes that I was not anticipating or planning on. Technology and information-sharing platforms had been kept out of my industry for years because of regulations. But industry-wide disruption was slowly breaking down walls, and technology was entering into every area of healthcare. Electronic medical records, patient information-sharing platforms, telemedicine, and mobile platforms began to replace methods that had been in place for years. The shift in how healthcare companies would engage with customers had fundamentally changed, and the days of delivering a message and having a customer take action based only on your efforts were over for good.

UNIVERSAL SENTIMENT

Around the same time I noticed these changes happening in my industry, I saw that the conditions were changing for companies within other industries as well. A universal shift in the way people bought was underway and happening to businesses regardless of the product, industry, or market. The business conditions as we knew them were changing, and it was time either to change or to become part of the past. I started to look closer at what was happening, talked to colleagues within other industries, and tried to figure out what the best course of action would be to overcome these new challenges. Switching jobs or companies would be like leaving one challenging situation and entering another. Being promoted to a new role within the same company would be hard since consolidation was happening at the top as well. Trying to switch to a new industry and try something new meant completely starting over with a new career.

PROFESSIONAL CHANGE

Knowing that the conditions would always be changing and that it would be hard if not impossible to predict or anticipate what would happen in the future, I thought the best thing to do would be to make a change that started with me. As I began to set out on this journey, I reconnected with a former professor of mine that happened to have a background in organization development. We grabbed coffee to talk about what was happening in business. My professor agreed that the conditions were changing within business at breakneck speeds and that it was up to the individual to make the necessary adjustments to stay ahead or fall behind. I started to formulate a plan about what I could do to survive these changes. Over the course of several subsequent coffee meetings with colleagues, I discussed how I could learn more about these new conditions and see if there was some way I could better manage what was happening around me.

2. A NEW DECISION

THINK DIFFERENT

Coming to the realization that I needed to change was hard. I had success selling and marketing a certain way, and I didn't think there was a better way to do it. To change, I needed to think differently and also start doing things differently. I felt a sense of urgency to make these changes happen, but it was hard to think differently because most of my colleagues and coworkers were experiencing the same thing, but still doing the same thing. People acknowledged the changes happening in the market, but everyone around me passed them off as short-term trends, thinking that the business would always go back to the way things had been. Most people had a fixed mindset toward these changes and continued to do things that had made them successful in the past. Many people saw doing anything new as either being too difficult or too risky. Without a good understanding of what was on the next horizon, most people just held on tight to what they knew and did little to think differently about their situations.

ACT DIFFERENT

Once I realized that I had to start thinking differently about my situation, I started to look for opportunities to begin making changes. Thinking differently was mentally challenging, but physically changing what I was doing was much harder. I had worked a certain way for years and had developed habits that were ingrained into what I did on a daily basis. I noticed myself reverting back to patterns and behaviors that once made me successful. Some patterns were as simple as checking email at a certain time every day or syncing my computer by 5:00 p.m. every night before I finished for the day. At other times, however, I noticed myself selling a certain way or taking a particular approach to how I was marketing or positioning our products. In those moments, I realized that so much of what I had done before was still with me and that I had to do something more significant to truly make a change.

TIME FOR CHANGE

After spending some time thinking through what I needed to change and attempting to make those changes, I knew that the only way to do something different would be to hit the reset button and take on a new challenge. As much as my company at the time made changes to adapt and meet the challenges of the new market, I soon realized that this process was going to take time, and there was a chance I would either be lost in the shuffle or come out on the other side in a place I didn't want to be. I started to plan my transition and talked to family and friends about how I would change. This process was also hard since the people closest to you are the most protective, and they want to keep you safe. The advice I got was to stay the course and play it safe. People kept telling me that everything would work out and that things would be fine. For a time, I refused the call and made the best of it. But over time, it was obvious that my situation would not change and that I could not continue in the direction I was headed.

3. MANAGE THE CHANGE

NEW CONDITIONS

After some thought and planning, I decided to make a change. I decided to take a journey that would give me insight into the new conditions and a better understanding of what was happening within sales and marketing. I wanted to step into the new market conditions, learn some new skills, and take on risk—something I had yet to do in my professional career. During this first part of the journey, I spent time exploring the new conditions, as if I were the surfer, paddling out into the conditions to try and catch some market waves. I would need a good understanding of what was happening, and I also wanted to see where my expertise stacked up within the market. Being in the conditions was the best way that I could build new skills to overcome these new challenges. Understanding the new conditions would be very important and the first step in my new journey.

NEW SKILLS

After understanding the new conditions, I would need to expand my sales and marketing capabilities. Over the years, I had been successful at selling and marketing products at retail and was able to do the same thing within healthcare. With both experiences, I had used traditional marketing and sales strategies as well as some of the new technology and platforms that were available. I had used CRM platforms, marketing automation, and mobile devices within both industries, but I knew that technology and information-sharing platforms would continue to change and that my traditional skills would need to be augmented with more modern marketing and updated sales abilities. It would be important to know what new skills I needed to add and how I could build those marketing and sales skills for the future. After understanding the market conditions and the new skills that I would need, it was then a matter of how much risk I was willing to take in order to make this change happen.

NEW RISK

Risk was something that, up until this point in my career, I had thought very little about. My previous roles at two companies over fifteen years had been very stable, and there was little to no professional disruption at all during that time. I was able to focus on learning the business and how to be successful within it. If I stuck to what I had done previously, it was relatively easy to be successful. However, if I made a change and decided to enter the new conditions, risk was going to be something that I faced on a more consistent basis. I was going from a safe, almost risk-free environment to a new way of thinking about business that was driven by risk. This change would be hard, but I was up for the challenge, and there was just as much risk staying where I was as there was with doing something new. I decided that regardless of the risk, I was going to make a change and would take on any challenge thrown in my direction. I was bringing a lot of risk into my personal life and professional career, but I was also ready for a new challenge.

SECTION II: NEW CHALLENGES FOR SALES AND MARKETING

"Organizations that destroy the status quo win. Whatever the status quo is, changing it gives you the opportunity to be remarkable."

—Seth Godin

THE NEW CHALLENGES

THE ABYSS

1. SYMBOLIC DROWNING

WORK STORY

Within a few months of each other, I had two experiences that challenged me both personally and professionally. I almost drowned trying to surf in the ocean, and I had reached a crossroads in my professional career. While one experience was life threatening and could have impacted my personal safety, the other was more challenging professionally and made me realize I had a lot of things to work through before I made a decision. Professionally, it was going to be tough to try to redefine who I was since my identity had been tied to my previous jobs for so long. I had developed a personal brand that defined me whether I liked it or not. Given the new challenges I experienced, I knew that I had to change, but that decision was overwhelming and reminded me of my experience in Malibu, being underwater and not knowing which direction was up or down.

SURF STORY

My surfing attempt at Malibu was a similar experience to what I had gone through professionally. There was more physical risk with surfing, but there were also mental challenges of planning for one outcome but experiencing a different result. I was well versed with boardsports and had been participating in them for years. It was easy for me to pick up skateboarding, snowboarding, and wakeboarding, but surfing was different. It was the first time I had felt like I had failed at a boardsport, and I was embarrassed by the results. The disappointment was a combination of underestimating the challenging conditions and not having the skills I needed to surf. I felt foolish for thinking it would be so easy and getting punished for it. The experience of being crushed by a large wave and pushed into the dark depths of the ocean was similar to what was happening to me professionally. I had now willingly put myself in a place where I would be challenged, beat up by the changing conditions, and would have to learn new skills to survive.

THE ABYSS

These two experiences happened within a few months of each other, and I was left to sort out what had happened as well as the results that my decisions had produced. Being in this unknown place was a heavy experience, but I knew I had a chance to right both wrongs and was willing to start the process of making amends with the ocean as well as the professional business world. I was going to pull myself out of this abyss, but I was also determined to take a new approach and look for ways to solve these problems. I wanted to be better equipped and more prepared when I encountered these obstacles again in the future. I had consulted with personal and professional connections, read books, and after weeks of searching, I still had not found a new way through these new challenges. Instead of using the traditional methods that did not create the dynamic I was looking for, I continued to contemplate how I would take the next steps in this journey.

2. THE ORDEAL

Innermost Cave

After going through these two challenging experiences, I was optimistic and felt motivated to tackle a new professional challenge. However, I felt held back, as though I was not free to make the decision I needed to, even though a professional change was the right thing to do. I was searching for affirmations and almost looking for ways to justify my decision to take a new journey. I needed to change, but I still was not ready to take the leap. Around this time, I was watching *The Dark Knight Rises*, and there is a scene in the movie where Bane breaks Batman's back and puts him into an underground prison—basically a hole in the ground. As Batman is recovering from his injuries, he hears a story of how a young child escaped from that prison, but only after the child climbed the wall without a rope and made the final leap without a safety line. Batman had tried to make the same leap a few times with the rope around his waist, but he only made it after he removed the rope and made the leap without it.

Willingness to Change

Although I was not in an underground prison or taking a leap for my personal freedom, metaphorically, I had to remove the safety line around my waist before I could make this change. The movie analogy was inspiring and showed me that if you're committed to taking on a new risk, you could free yourself from your current situation and make a change. I removed the safety line and said to myself, "I don't know what will happen, but I'm prepared to take on this new challenge and will face the obstacles in a way that I had not approached them before." It was liberating and terrifying at the same time, but it felt like the decision I needed to make in order to force this change. I made a decision to commit to the change. After the decision, and now out of the cave, I took the steps to embrace the conditions and understand what was happening, then I developed a new process to manage it.

Self-Annihilation

Outside of my inner cave and after making the leap into the new conditions, I knew that the person I was now would soon be a distant memory. As I began to head in this new direction, I started to shed the previous me. I started to mentally discard the ideas that I had used in the past and physically dispose of the possessions that tied me to the previous way of doing things. This sounds extreme, but I needed to purge anything that reinforced my old habits, old ideas, or made me physically feel like the old John. I got rid of clothing, books, and even rearranged my home office to mark the beginning of this new journey. I knew that my old possessions could not hang around because they would undermine what I was trying to do, and that I could not make the mental change without making a set of physical changes too. I saw these as changes designed to annihilate the old and build up the new.

3. THE RENEWING ACT

METAMORPHOSIS

As I started to make the physical changes to my environment, I could feel a sense of change and forward movement. I had new energy for the challenges ahead, but it was balanced by the concern for what I might face and whether or not I would be ready for what I encountered. During the first few months of the journey, I was really just focused on making the transition and adapting to the change. I had put myself into these new conditions on my own, and at this point, I was just trying to manage the change and understand what it would now be like without the safety net of an organization underneath me. There were a few tough months during the transition, since I was really just trying to change myself and had not yet ventured too far into the new conditions. There were hiccups and missteps along the way, but I knew that with success comes failure, and this was part of the process. I had made the decision to change, so I took my bumps and knew that I would need to make these changes in order to be successful.

REBIRTH OF SKILLS

For so long, I had been working for an organization and really got locked into a certain mindset about my skills and capabilities. I had built up a certain set of skills while inside organizations, and they served me well within that internal system. But I noticed right away that a different set of skills was needed for the new conditions. I had to break away from my old mindset about my skills being static or fixed and approach the development of those skills from the standpoint of being more fluid and evolving. I wanted to explore the new conditions and find out for myself what skills and capabilities would be needed in these new conditions and also in the future. I realized that my skills would need to go through a rebirth and that I would need to use my previous skills to build and develop new ones. I had a foundation to build upon, but my professional development would be the primary focus of this new journey.

BORN AGAIN

This decision to change was a renewing act. It was both a physical and mental rebirth that felt as though I was in a new world with more options and more control. As I started to understand the new conditions and the new skills I would need, I realized that if I wanted to do something new, I really just had to do it. I also realized that I was only held back by the constraints that I put on myself. If I could think about something new to do, it was really just a matter of doing it. This approach created a whole new relationship with risk that I was exploring, as I used to think of risk as being self-limiting. I now realized that I would need to explore new risk if I was going to change who I was. My only risk was whether or not I was willing to make an attempt at something new, and if I could live with the professional or personal embarrassment I might feel if I failed.

THE JOURNEY

1. 1. THE KNOWN

KNOWN CONDITIONS

As I began this new journey on my own, I first started to explore what was known. There were a set of beliefs I had about myself, the business world, and how I conducted myself in it. After seeing what was new, I realized that I somewhat limited myself by being content with where I was professionally and had worked a certain way for so long that it had become my known reality. I was in a bubble and had created imaginary boundaries for myself. As I began this journey, this was true for most everyone I spoke to. We all had a certain viewpoint of the market, how a company fit into that market, and our place as individuals within it. Organizations and professionals all fill certain roles or play their part—just as I had done for years. When I realized I had been simply playing a role and not proactively exploring what was new, my first reaction was frustration. I thought about how I had been stifled by my perceptions of what was possible in the conditions and how it may have negatively impacted my success.

KNOWN SKILLS

When I talked with organizations and professionals while on this journey, they explained their skills and capabilities in very pragmatic terms. You either had a certain skill or capability or you didn't. Professionals felt as if they were forced into a role based on their experience. If you had not spent any time doing a specific role, it was unthinkable that you could do that job. And most professionals were not given a chance at a new role without receiving that experience somewhere else first. It was an odd predicament and really challenging for professionals who wanted to do something new but were stuck because of very traditional mindsets about skills and capabilities. Professionals sticking to what they had done previously and to what was known versus taking on the risks with something new was a mindset about holding onto the past and not progressively thinking about the future.

KNOWN RISK

Taking professional risk has historically been avoided, and business leaders generally steered clear of anything seen as different from what they were currently doing. In talking with organizations, I noticed skepticism around unproven and untested ideas, concepts, processes, and systems. Anything new was dismissed as trendy, and teams with new ideas were often told by leadership, "That wouldn't work here." Even if processes or systems were not producing the intended results, new methods were still avoided, and managers, teams, and companies would grind out poor results, using tired and old ideas. There was a fixed mindset against anything new, and systems supported the traditional ways of doing business. If an organization had worked a certain way for years, it seemed like it would take an intervention for things to change. There were organizations that had the resources and finances to invest in new systems, but the fear of professional risk and change was the major deterrent to trying anything new.

2. THE UNKNOWN

UNKNOWN CONDITIONS

After continuing to meet with business leaders while on my journey, I noticed a set of shared experiences among almost all organizations. There were three main ideas that came up time and time again during our discussions. The first idea was that the external market conditions had fundamentally changed. This topic came up during every conversation I had, and leadership identified what was changing in the markets or negatively impacting success. Technology had changed how customers were buying in markets, and companies were finding that they needed to better understand how new platforms and technologies were giving their customers the upper hand. Potential customers had access to more information, and most were savvy enough to make purchase decisions on their own, independent of marketers or sellers. Competitors were using technology platforms to increase their reach among customers and finding new opportunities where others were not. The external market conditions had changed and most organizations were not embracing those changes.

UNKNOWN SKILLS

The second idea was that a new set of skills and capabilities would be needed for these new conditions, including new skills for the individual but also a new set of capabilities for organizations as well. Leadership was no longer investing in training around new skills for individuals, and organizations were not creating development programs for enhancing the capabilities of the organization. Companies would hire from outside the organization to bring in new skills rather than develop talent from the inside. This approach created groups of individuals that possessed the desired new skill, but it never translated to organizational capabilities because once those people left the organization, that skill or capability left as well.

Leaders did not have a mindset toward development and were simply poaching talent without developing their people from the inside. This thinking was a short-term strategy, but long term, it presented a new challenge, as organizations started to buckle when those new skills were needed.

UNKNOWN RISK

The third idea was that individuals and organizations had a new relationship with risk that was more extreme than anything business professionals had experienced before. Organizations that were not embracing the new external conditions and not adding new skills or capabilities were also facing new risks by not adapting to the changes in markets. Leadership relied on the status quo and showed a lack of confidence in how to overcome marketing and sales challenges in new conditions. As a result, marketing and sales initiatives never produced the desired results, and organizations were stuck in cycles of doing the same thing over and over without ever achieving an improved result. Companies did not see that not changing was the new, real risk and that holding onto the past would be a death sentence. After experiencing the challenges within the new conditions for myself and seeing organizations that were struggling, I started to narrow the focus on these three areas and to explore each of them further.

3. THE JOURNEY

WHAT I DID

As I continued to speak with business leaders about each of the three areas, I soon realized that these were common challenges to everyone. Regardless of the industry, the specific market, or the product or service, business leaders were all experiencing these three challenges in some form or another. The more information and feedback I collected, the clearer it was that these ideas were universal challenges to anyone in business at that moment. On my journey, I spent my time with organizations, navigating these new conditions, identifying the new skills and organizational capabilities that would be needed to succeed, but also exploring ways for organizations to do things that were new and feel more confident about how they could take on risk. I used the three areas as a way to assess how company leadership within organizations were embracing the new conditions, how they were progressing their current skills, and if they were willing to risk a change that would allow them to do something new.

WHO I TALKED TO

After identifying the three areas, I met with business leaders within organizations who were CEOs, on executive leadership teams, and anyone who was working within marketing or sales. I wanted to gain a high-level perspective of what was happening within organizations and understand their challenges in implementing new sales and marketing initiatives. I specifically focused on marketing and sales because the new challenges were severely impacting these two areas. Technology, information-sharing platforms, and software were impacting marketing and sales the most, but these areas also had the biggest impact on an organization's bottom line. They are also the main revenue drivers within any organization. I did a series of discovery workshops with the concepts to figure out how certain organizations were able to overcome the new challenges and be successful.

WHAT I LEARNED

It was clear from my conversations with business leaders that the three areas were universal challenges. Each organization was dealing with these challenges at some level and looking for a better way to manage what was happening in their markets and also inside their own organizations. As I worked with companies to understand how they were overcoming the challenges, I started to identify the successful methods that were being used—a set of best practices that were universal and consistent among the successful organizations. The more I worked with marketing and sales leadership, the more I saw that the organizations having success knew the market conditions, were constantly adding new skills and capabilities, but were also willing to try new things in order to improve on what they had done previously. These organizations had internal processes to support their strategies, had developed incentives to explore risk, and had created reward systems that supported new change.

THE DISCOVERY

1. THE LEARNING

THE PEOPLE

Over a two-year period of exploring these three concepts with hundreds of organizations and business leaders, I discovered that the challenges were universal and common across all areas of business, regardless of the industry. I also realized that a set of organizations had not only figured out how to survive in these new conditions, but how to thrive in them. The successful companies all used a similar approach to overcome the new challenges, and this process had less to do with the size of the company, revenues, or the talent, but more to do with the strategy and mindset as they related to their markets, skills, and unique challenges. The successful companies focused on doing things differently than most of their contemporaries and had a process for overcoming challenges. They approached business differently than the organizations that used traditional ideas or methods, and they thumbed their collective noses at the status quo whenever they could.

THE PROCESS

The successful companies were in different industries and markets, but they were all similar in the way they handled the new challenges. Each company had a process of evaluating what was happening outside the organization, a way to assess what skills they needed inside the organization to tackle those new external challenges, and a tolerance for risk that allowed the organization to test ideas as well as bring innovative new strategies to the markets. As I documented the processes used by the successful organizations, it was clear that each company had a unique way of approaching the new challenges and used repeatable processes to overcome them. External evaluations of the market conditions happened every three to six months or more if changes occurred because of new products or new regulations. Internal assessments of skills happened every six to twelve months, with development initiatives happening every three months. New ideas were tested and prototyped before they went live, with failure being a common occurrence and widely accepted during the process.

THE RESULTS

Similarities existed among the successful companies in terms of a process, and they were also able to have consistent results from their efforts. The successful organizations stood out for how they were approaching the new challenges, but their distinction also came through in their results. These organizations understood the conditions, had a mindset toward new skills, and were willing, more so than others, to try something new and to be OK with failing in the short term in order to achieve long-term results. For the successful organizations, the results were increased revenues, increased profitability, and improved employee engagement. However, there were also results that you could not measure in dollars or percentages—the satisfaction of being tested, trying something new, and finding a new way to solve a new problem or challenge. These were the kinds of "results" that organizations really liked to talk about and that were the main motivators for them to achieve success again.

2. THE REALIZATION

THE COMPANIES

In working with the successful companies, I started to notice a set of similar principles that each of them shared in relation to the new challenges. Given my recent surf experience in Malibu, I started to think about the successful companies and how they were similar to the surfers I had watched from the beach. The realization grew the more I explored the parallels between the two groups and how they did similar things in terms of how they achieved success. The companies that were different from the status quo and were repeatedly successful had a set of principles similar to those of surfers. They embraced the market conditions and were always out there and in them. Their mindset for skills was focused on learning and always progressing their capabilities. They were also willing to take on risk and fail in order to find new success. The organizations that fared well in the new conditions outperformed those that stuck with the status quo and were very similar to surfers in their approach to skills, mindset, and risk.

THE SURFERS

The surfers I saw out in the ocean at Malibu embodied how the top organizations approached their business and also how they achieved success. I noticed that a set of principles made the surfers successful as well. It was easy to tell who was knowledgeable about the conditions, and this was also a good predictor of who was going to catch the waves. The good surfers knew the conditions, where the waves were breaking and how to find the right spots to catch them, and when to paddle or when to rest and wait. They also knew their individual skills and capabilities as well as which waves were going to be easy for them to ride and which waves might be too much for them to handle. Finally, the good surfers knew when and how to explore uncertainty by taking calculated risks and building up to more challenging waves after testing themselves on the smaller ones first.

THE SIMILARITIES

A lot of similarities existed between the successful companies and the good surfers. You could tell that they just got it and had strong knowledge about the conditions and their skills. They knew how to push themselves and progress their surfing in the face of risk. For the business leaders who were successful, the same was true. They were willing to take a look outside of their organizations and understand what was happening within their market. Their mindset was similar to the surfers in that they were progressive and always thinking about their next trick or next wave. They approached risk by thinking of it as a compass to point them in the direction they needed to go. Both the surfers and successful business leaders were unique in how they approached their sport or business in a way that was different from the status quo. Just as a good surfer is distinguished from other surfers, the successful organizations distinguished themselves from other companies in that they were the "good surfers" of the business world.

3. THE PARALLELS

MY EXPERIENCES

My two separate experiences, one personal and one professional, began to come together as I drew more and more parallels between them. The experience of a failed surf attempt followed up by a failed product launch actually brought new clarity to both situations. They were different in that I experienced each in separate areas of my life, but similar in that the end result was unexpected and not intended. The more I thought about each experience, the more I considered surfers as the model for success. I started to see where I had gone wrong with my own surf experience and how I could approach that same situation again in the future and come out with a desired result. I also used the parallel to see how the successful companies were different than those that focused on maintaining the status quo. I realized that there could be a way for me to use what I had learned from surfers and the successful companies to help others overcome similar challenges.

THE PARALLELS

There were parallels between what the business leaders and the surfers did that made each of them successful in their sport or in business. The parallels were a set of actions, a mindset, and an approach—a set of principles or best practices for overcoming new challenges. I created each new principle and mapped out the best approach for the surfer and then found the similar approach for the business professional. For example, "this is what the surfer does and how he or she is successful" and "this is what the successful company does, which embodies the new principle of the surfer." For each of the three main challenges within surfing, there is a corresponding principle that creates a bridge to how a business leader can overcome that same challenge in the professional world. The surfer is the guide, not only identifying the new challenges but also serving as the model for how to overcome the obstacles. By using the three principles, a business leader can overcome any market challenge and be successful just like the surfer.

THE PRINCIPLES

The parallels between surfing and business are the foundation for the three new principles. The principles are common to surfers and foundational to their sport. For business professionals, they are new concepts that create a process for evaluating and developing ways to overcome challenging situations. The three principles are: 1) Embrace the Changing Conditions: just like the surfer, you must know the conditions and know what to expect, and to understand the conditions you need to be out there and put yourself directly in them. 2) Adopt a Progression-Based Mindset: like the surfer, you need to constantly improve your individual professional skills and identify ways to improve your organization's capabilities. 3) Use Risk as a Compass: take action in the face of uncertainty or fear, just like the surfer who continues to paddle out into the water, even though there are sharks, rocks, and hazards around every wave. All three in combination with one another provide a way for professionals to manage the new conditions and find success.

UNIVERSAL LESSON 5

WHAT I LEARNED ABOUT SURFERS

1. EMBRACE THE CONDITIONS

SURFERS USE TECHNOLOGY

There are three things that I learned from watching the surfers in Malibu. The first lesson is how surfers embrace the changing conditions. Surfers don't have a universal field, court, or rink in which they practice their sport. The size of the waves, depth of the water, and the conditions they surf in are always different and always changing. Trying to manage the changing conditions from surf spot to surf spot can be challenging. Fortunately, new technology has made the conditions more manageable for surfers. Using technology to track weather and waves has become a standard practice in surfing. Professionals use surf reports to find out where waves are breaking and can use hyperaccurate reports about whether or not there will be waves. Surf reports have revolutionized the sport, giving surfers the ability to travel the world and make the most of conditions that might otherwise have been missed without the capabilities of new technology.

SURFERS GET OUT THERE

The second lesson is that surfers embrace the conditions and get out there and into the water. Even with technology to predict waves, the surfer still needs to be in the water in a position to catch a wave. Surfers paddle out regardless of the current conditions. Surfers scan the horizon and watch for waves to build and break just offshore. Surfers are always in the line-up and put themselves where the action is—not by waiting for waves from the shore. This situation is unique and different from most sports where the conditions and environmental elements are always the same. You know there will always be a goal, net, or hoop at the other end of the field or court and that the other team will show up to play the game. With surfing, you need to be willing to get out there, even if the conditions are not perfect. For surfers, it's about understanding the conditions, knowing how the ocean works, and having the patience for waves to make their way to shore.

SURFERS ARE PATIENT

The final thing that surfers do to embrace the conditions is wait. Surfers are patient, and they will wait for hours to catch waves. Surfers wait in the cold ocean water, paddle in challenging conditions, and wait for the next opportunity to catch a wave. Surfers may wait for hours to catch a five-second ride to shore. This infrequency tests their patience, physical abilities, and mental fortitude to sit in the water for that long without having success. They have developed the patience necessary to wait for waves by focusing on preparing for opportunities to catch their wave and not just any wave that rolls toward shore. Surfers are patient when they wait, but they are also patient in how they pick and choose opportunities to catch waves. They wait patiently for a wave that fits their abilities and offers the best ride that their skills and abilities can handle.

2. MINDSET FOR NEW SKILLS

SURFERS UNDERSTAND PROGRESSION

The second lesson is that surfers have a progression-based mindset and understand the importance of adding new skills. The mindset of surfers and how they approach the sport is founded on progression or an approach to acquiring and learning new skills. Progression is commonly defined as progress or forward movement, but surfers apply this word to how they acquire and learn new skills. Progression is also fundamental to all boardsports, including skateboarding, snowboarding, and wakeboarding, but has its roots in surfing. Surfers understand that progression is important for always trying to improve upon what they are doing. They are always trying to do a trick better or to add to what they have done before. For example, when surfers began to do aerial maneuvers on waves, the sport "progressed" in terms of what was possible because surfers were able to catch air, add grabs, and learn new tricks by progressing the sport through aerial maneuvers.

THE SURFER MINDSET

Surfers have what's called a "progression-based" mindset. Progression is also a major part of the surf culture and how surfers think about improving themselves within their sport. With a progression-based mindset, surfers are always improving upon what they did previously as well as improving their skills and capabilities. This type of mindset is different and novel to surfing. Athletes in other sports acquire and master a skill, then usually stop there. Surfers build skills progressively in order to acquire new ones, and they use this mindset to keep motivating themselves to improve. Progression is also integrated into surf contests and one of the ways that judges pick winners. Judges look at how surfers are progressing their tricks from heat to heat and who is doing the most progressive maneuvers on their boards wave after wave. Surfers push themselves using a progression-based mindset, but the context within surfing also supports progression within the sport.

SURFERS PROGRESS

Surfers acquire and then build upon their current skills. They are continually building upon what they have done before and use the accomplishment of acquiring a new skill as a launching point for learning something new. Few sports and few athletes progress this way, but for surfers, it's important to the long-term success of their sport. Today's surfers can't surf the way the pros did even ten years ago. The boards are now smaller and lighter, and the technology is better, which has helped surfers to progress the sport toward bigger waves. Breaks that were once thought to be too sketchy are now being ridden. The popularity of surfing has exploded, gone mainstream, and will be an Olympic sport in 2020. The sport is popular because it attracts participants who want to learn, progress, and continually accomplish something new in their sport.

3. USE RISK AS A COMPASS

SURFERS EXPECT RISK

The third lesson is the willingness to explore and take on risk. Surfers expose themselves to a tremendous amount of risk. Beyond the basic physical injuries that can happen as a result of an athletic sport, surfers face another set of risks that are even more hazardous. They can become injured just like any other athlete and blow out a knee, pick up nicks and scrapes, as well as experience head injuries or concussions from their sport. However, a surfer must face another level of life-threatening risks. The ocean boasts more predators than any other environment on the planet. Surfers willingly put themselves in harm's way by attempting to paddle into these

untamed conditions and face threats from animals that mistake them for an easy snack. Sharks are the most menacing risk that any surfer will face in the ocean. Including personal injury and natural predators, surfers expect the risks and use them to push them in the right direction.

SURFERS EXPLORE RISK

Surfers not only expect risk, but they also explore it. In some cases, they try to exploit it. Take big wave surfing as an example. Surfers seek out, hunt for, and find the biggest waves on the planet to test their abilities. With smaller waves come more style, trick progression, and skill, but with big wave surfing it's about paddling into and charging massive waves. Conditions that any other normal, non-surfing person would try to avoid at all costs, surfers explore with pleasure. Surfers continually pursue larger, more challenging waves to progress their skills and abilities. With ever-increasing wave size providing a ladder of progression, surfers challenge themselves every time they try to tackle a bigger, more massive wave. Surfers build new skills each and every time they ride a wave, and they explore new risks in order to improve. There is a lot of intent behind their actions, and this intentional exposure to risk sets them apart from athletes in other disciplines.

SURFERS RISK TO PROGRESS

Surfers always expect risk to be associated with riding waves. Surfers need to explore risk and pursue it if they want to progress in their sport. Much of what surfers do outside of the sport in terms of training and preparation is designed to lower the risks and make progression possible. Surfers train on land to become stronger, training muscles that are needed for when a wave breaks. For the surfer, risk and progression go hand in hand. You can't have one without the other. In order to become better and progress in surfing, you have to be comfortable with risk, know how to explore it, and do so willingly. Surfers open themselves up to the risks that are inherent in the conditions and explore risk with the expectation that they will survive whatever the ocean can throw at them to live and surf another day. Risk is part of the process that leads toward the path of progression and helps the surfer get better at what they do.

WHAT I LEARNED ABOUT SALES AND MARKETING

1. CUSTOMER POWER

CUSTOMERS HAVE THE POWER

Just as the surfer faces the challenges from the ever-changing ocean conditions, the business leader constantly needs to add new skills and explore new risk in order to succeed in new conditions. The days of relying on past skills and abilities are over, and a new approach is needed. The advent of new technology within sales and marketing has given customers buying power, and organizations are no longer in control of the buying process. They no longer have the power they had even just a few years ago. Technology and information-sharing platforms have put customers in the driver's seat and armed them with vast amounts of information that they can now use to make purchase decisions. The barriers to knowledge have been lowered, and anyone with a smartphone can find information about a product or service, shop for the best deal, and ultimately circumvent a traditional marketing and sales process to buy.

THE CUSTOMER'S NEW JOURNEY

The decision journey for customers to make a purchase decision is different. In the past, the process to market and sell a product or service to a buyer was linear from marketing to sales. It was described as a "funnel" where a top-down approach would push information to customers through channels. Organizations would systematically move potential customers through a purchase decision in a very strategic and organized way. In the current conditions, however, customers can jump into the process anywhere along that path and take themselves on a self-guided journey to make a purchase decision. Customers no longer rely on anyone from an organization until much later in the process, with the role of sales becoming more concierge than salesman or woman. This new journey has put organizations in a tough position since they are now responsible for educating customers and moving them through a unique process to make a decision.

CUSTOMER EXPECTATIONS

This new journey has also created a new set of expectations from customers. They have the power to shop for products and services on multiple platforms to find the best deals and are no longer forced to buy from a single source. Customers have access to more information and want greater transparency in terms of cost and price. They expect more control in the buying process and are leveraging this kind of information to make better purchase decisions, which has put pressure on sellers to offer the best deal up front. Customers have a better understanding of the buying process and are finding ways to unbundle services and find exactly what they want. Rather than going to a traditional brick-and-mortar bank to set up a payment service for a business, customers can now find companies that offer software platforms at a fraction of the cost. The expectations of customers have changed, and organizations need to adapt accordingly.

2. NEED FOR NEW SKILLS

ORGANIZATIONS AND SKILLS

Along my journey, I noticed that the organizations that had been around the longest were the most tied to the old way of doing things. Newer companies that have formed within the last three to five years were able to build their organizations with the latest technology and newest software, and they also leveraged some of the latest trends. Companies that were built on traditional sales and marketing skills had the hardest time acquiring new organizational capabilities. Organizations were in a challenging spot because if they lacked certain skills, they needed to hire new employees and staff to add those skills in-house. However, leadership struggled to develop those skills into organizational capabilities and cycled through employees with those skills, instead of developing them to remain at the organization long term. Organizations, just like employees, need to think about their skills as fluid and ever-changing—just like the conditions they are working in. It can be an uphill battle if organizational leadership doesn't understand the new conditions or chooses to ignore the challenges and just hope that things will improve.

ORGANIZATIONS AND MINDSET

In order to make changes and develop new skills, the collective mindset of the organization has to be open to what's needed for the organization, but also to what's new and changing markets. Some organizations have a resistance mindset or an aversion to anything new. New can be expensive to an organization and can even cost someone a job if not executed correctly. The organizations that were struggling were all locked into a mindset of the past and relying on previous success, not thinking about what was next or how they could better solve their customers' problems. They were locked into a mentality where change was not encouraged or supported by the organization, and that made it hard for the organization to progress or move forward. Organizations that had a hard time with the new challenges also experienced frustration among their team members who saw the need for change and wanted to make improvements but were forced to "toe the company line" due to the organization's fixed mindset.

ORGANIZATIONS AND PROGRESSION

Companies that did not add new skills and capabilities on a consistent basis all had employees that suffered as a result. Teams did not feel challenged or were "held back" from making more strategic decisions. Organizations that did not change their mindset or meet the new challenges all had customers that suffered as well. Offering the same product or service the same way, year after year, and not evolving or progressing how that product or service solves problems for clients makes it hard for consumers to connect with what an organization is offering. Markets change, and customers' needs change as well. The need for new organizational skills and a new mindset will force organizations to rethink how they are connecting with their customers. Customers are changing and evolving, adapting to new technology, and living their lives in new ways. If a product offering is not progressing to match the needs of customers or the way customers now buy, companies will struggle to find success.

3. RISK AND UNEXPECTED RESULTS

ORGANIZATIONS AND RISK

The organizations that did not take the time to understand the new conditions and the new way that customers buy struggled to find success and had unintended or unexpected results. They were not willing to risk learning about the new dynamics in their markets and were not willing to risk the time to figure out new solutions to these challenges. Companies that struggled continued to use the same strategies that worked in markets years ago and failed to adapt to the new conditions, not realizing that what they were doing was not going to work in the new conditions and that the results would not be what was expected. For organizations, this was damaging and also hurt the psyche of the marketer or sales professional doing the work. Organizations were not taking the time to ask customers questions about how they were finding out about their products and what considerations they were making when it came to making a final purchase decision. The companies that were not willing to risk doing something new were hurt the most and struggled to produce results because of this resistance.

ORGANIZATIONS AND SKILLS

The companies that did not understand the conditions or try to develop their skills and capabilities to meet the demands of the new conditions struggled to find sales and marketing success. Organizations that did find success were continually evaluating individual skills and organizational capabilities on a regular basis. Challenges and obstacles became impassable when teams were not staffed with the right talent and expertise for the new conditions. Companies that did not add new training or development programs to build new skills found that results were hard to predict and did not meet organizational expectations. Companies that did not add new skills or take risks in order to change fell behind the market and competition. The companies that did succeed, however, added new skills and had results that met or exceeded expectations. It was clear that the organizations that took risks in order to change had the best results.

ORGANIZATIONS AVOID RISK

The organizations that did not understand the new conditions and did not add new skills put leadership in the position of playing defense instead of offense. The mindset or mentality was focused on risk aversion or an aversion to anything outside the comfort zone of the organization. Leadership had built up a tolerance to change, and preserving the status quo became the new norm. Aversion to risk had become part of company culture, and new ideas or innovations were met with the classic, "We've never done that before," or, "That's not how we do it here." The organizations where leadership had this approach to risk tended to "play it safe" and avoided anything that might upset the status quo within the organization, even if it meant achieving poor results. The organizations that struggled had no incentives to change, and maintaining the status quo was the measurement of success. For leadership at these organizations, trying to overcome the new challenges was like a shock to the organizational system, with marketing and sales bearing the brunt of this crushing blow.

A UNIVERSAL JOURNEY

1. UNIVERSAL EXPERIENCE

PERSONAL EXPERIENCE

We have all experienced challenges in our personal and professional lives—like I experienced while surfing and trying to navigate the new business conditions. Often there are challenges we did not expect. We are not prepared, and we end up experiencing frustration because of the results. We experience failure trying to overcome a new challenge, but where we make errors is in using what worked for us in the past. I would guess that this happens quite frequently and that most people are caught off guard when it comes to taking on some of life's most unexpected challenges. This is a universal experience that we have all encountered before. We are blindsided by an unexpected challenge or change, and it leaves us wondering, "What just happened? How did I not see this coming?" The failure is personal, but it's an experience that's universal, and we can all relate to it. Think of an experience when you wanted to make a change or do something new. There is a good chance that what you experienced was not what you planned for, and you most likely encountered some kind of mental or physical obstacle that was hard to overcome.

CHALLENGES AND OBSTACLES

We will continue to experience new challenges in the business world. There will always be challenges or obstacles, and as the rate of change increases with technology and information-sharing platforms, we are opening ourselves up to more and more of these situations. Instead of experiencing a life or job change once in a career or once in a lifetime, the rate will exponentially grow, and we will be faced with challenges and obstacles more frequently than ever before. It's hard to predict how often we will experience this type of change, but estimates have marketers experiencing job changes every forty-four months, which means that every three and a half years, a marketer will have a new role professionally. It used to be that business professionals would not have a single change within their careers, but the reality within business is that changes will happen more often and will be more disruptive to our lives.

OVERCOMING CHANGE

Now and in the future, we will all be looking for ways to manage these new challenges better and will try not be wiped out by them. We will need new ways to manage changes and to prepare ourselves for market waves and new strategies to feel confident in the decisions that we're making. Since the challenges and obstacles are universal, so is the journey that we all go through when we have these experiences. But how we solve these challenges for ourselves and for the organizations we work for is a different story. Since there is a shared experience with new challenges, there is no reason why there can't be a shared process for overcoming them as well. Up until now, there has not been a model or process to manage these new changes or a method to help individuals manage, survive, and also thrive in them.

2. UNIVERSAL CHALLENGES

NEW JOURNEY

Now that we are all on this new journey to overcome business challenges, we need a way to approach them without suffering major setbacks and also a repeatable process that we can consistently use over time. Organizations that have not yet experienced the challenges soon will; it's just a matter of time. This is a universal change within business and a universal experience that we will all need to embrace. We will need to embrace new market changes, identify new skills, and manage new risk on a regular basis. Customers are experiencing a new journey in how they search, shop for, and make purchase decisions for products and services. We are both experiencing these changes together, just from different perspectives. In order for organizations to manage the new conditions better, the first step will be aligning with the customer's new decision journey.

NEW SKILLS

In order to meet the customer demands of this new journey, a close look at current skills is necessary as well as a process to evaluate which new skills will be the most helpful. The days of basking in previous successes or relying on skills of the past are over. Organizations and leaders will need to consistently assess how they are marketing and selling products and if they are offering services in a way that meets the needs of customers. Skills and capabilities will need to evolve, but so will the mindset around the process of adding them as well. Adopting a progression-based mindset toward skills and capabilities will be needed since skills are no longer static but in a constant flux within organizations. This is another universal experience that we all share—trying to get better at what we do. There has not been a process that encourages this kind of mindset in order to meet the demands of our new business environment. Traditional development methods tend to focus on "playing to our strengths," but what's needed to meet the new demands is far different and much more demanding.

NEW RISK

With the new challenges and the need for new skills comes risk. Risk is now a universal experience that we will all share in what we do professionally. In the past, business professionals have remained immune from risk because of the insulation a lot of organizations provide. Companies that have good products or services, along with the support of talented employees, have been insulated from change and have had little to no disruptions in their markets. But as customers continue to drive market changes, organizations that were once insulated could be exposed to new threats and challenges that they have not experienced before. In order to meet the new challenges and overcome them, organizations will need to step out into the new conditions, armed with new skills, and also take a new approach to risk. In the new conditions, business leaders will have to keep putting themselves in harm's way to overcome challenges and succeed.

3. UNIVERSAL PRINCIPLES

EMBRACE THE CONDITIONS

As business leaders, we all share the experiences of what it's like in the new market conditions. There's a need for a new mindset around skills and also a need for a new relationship with risk. Having a universal process not only makes sense but is necessary if we want to survive wave after wave of new change, but also ride some of those waves successfully back into shore. The comparison of surfers to business professionals helps make sense of the new challenges, but it also provides us with a way to use surfing principles as a new business process for success. There's not another sport where the conditions are as challenging, where a specific mindset around skills is needed, or where the consequences for failure are as severe. Surfing is a good analogy for the way business leaders will need to approach sales and marketing in the future. It also provides us with a set of principles that leadership can use to guide their organizations through the process of finding success in changing markets by using the natural momentum or waves within markets to overcome new challenges.

PROGRESSION-BASED MINDSET

Traditionally, we have thought of our individual skills and organizational capabilities as fixed. Meaning, we acquired new ones through years of experience on the job and focused on that one set of skills and mastering them before adding new ones. In the new conditions, leadership will need to think about skills as progression-based and not fixed. Teams will not only need to develop a set of skills and adapt to the changing conditions, but also continue to develop those skills over time. The new mindset that leadership needs to have is that the organization needs to change as the market changes. A marketer or sales professional will need to change with the customers to meet their specific needs and solve their problems as they change as well. The surfer can serve as the new model of the mindset needed, and the idea of progression-based skills will be necessary in the new conditions.

RISK AS A COMPASS

As leaders progress their skills and capabilities, risk will be a constant factor in their failure or success. In the new conditions, failure will happen more often and more consistently. Actual moments of defined success will happen less and less—more like a progression of small successes over time and smaller gains as a result of focused effort versus big wins. Sales and marketing leaders will need to use risk as a compass. Meaning they will need to push in the direction of new challenges in order to be successful. The conditions are calling for it, and the organizations that encourage the exploration of risk will be successful because of it. Up until this point, there has not been a process that explores risk as the gateway to business success. However, what makes this approach different is that it's about intentionally exposing yourself to risk in order to progress. Just like the surfer who paddles out into the waves each and every day, the business leader will need to make peace with risk and face it more and more to find success.

THE THREE PRINCIPLES OF THE SURFER

WHY SURFERS?

1. THE BUSINESS OF SURFING

SURFERS AND BUSINESS

To help business leaders manage the changing conditions, the surfer and the three principles create a new process to solve market challenges. The surfer analogy is a way to help organizations break away from the traditional methods of solving problems and embrace a new way of approaching market challenges. The three principles are rooted in the idea that business leaders now need to be more like the surfer and approach business challenges by embracing the conditions, changing their mindset toward skills, and using risk exploration to find success. Be more like surfers by learning how they approach new challenges, and use the three principles as a guide to solving problems. Just as surfers "ride a wave" in the ocean, business leaders can use the principles as a process and discover a new set of benefits by adopting these behaviors.

A NEW APPROACH

The three principles are a new approach to managing the

changing business conditions, using the natural momentum in markets along with an organization's strengths to find success. Too much of what we focus on with processes and methods is based on trying to improve our weaknesses or deficiencies. Improving our weaknesses is oftentimes not impactful because it's hard to overcome the things that we are not naturally good at. We value action over inactivity, even if it's misdirected, and we are reactive versus proactive with our approach to new challenges and obstacles because it's easier. We value "hard work" and long hours instead of strategic consideration, and we try to have overworked teams do more without any thought to the actual benefit those additional hours might bring. More work has become "better work," but this approach doesn't offer a realistic solution when business leaders are faced with new challenges, and putting more hours against a problem will not make it go away. The three principles create a new approach to thinking strategically about business challenges and can help organizations focus on the important work instead of doing more of it.

USING THE PRINCIPLES

There is a lot of doubt, anxiety, and concern about how to solve the new business challenges we are facing. The three principles will provide you with examples of how surfers overcome challenges and how you can overcome new business challenges as well. For surfers, there is a set of principles that can be applied to situations regardless of the conditions. Surfers increase their chances of success by using the principles every time they surf. The same can be true for business leaders. The examples that follow are from research on how organizations have used these three principles to be successful. These proven strategies will provide you with innovative ideas that can be applied to what you are trying to accomplish within your organization. The principles present a new way to overcome market challenges and build new skills, as well as a process for testing new ideas in the face of risk.

2. THE PRINCIPLES AND BUSINESS

REVELATIONS

As I worked with the three principles and applied them to business situations, I could see that there was a natural connection and business leaders were receptive to the concepts. The principles helped change how organizations viewed their markets, and we found ways to make strategic changes in how they sold or marketed products. The revelation occurred when I regularly heard things such as, "We just need to get in the water," or, "We're still on the beach," and even, "We need some new tricks." In my discussions with business leaders, we talked about the challenges in business terms but used the examples from surfing to outline the strategies and tactics that organizations wanted to explore. The surf concepts allowed me to have a low-pressure conversation with leadership, and the process created some novelty around talking about the problems that organizations were facing.

FINDING SUCCESS

Marketing and sales leadership explored the ideas that came out of our discussions about the three principles. The process put new challenges into a different context and liberated leadership from old ideas by giving them confidence in new ones. The three principles became the bridge from challenges or problems to an entirely new and unique set of solutions that were customized to their organization. The organizations that were successful with the principles had a new contempt and disdain for the status quo. They used the principles to identify old ideas and clear out the "deadwood" that had held them back from exploring new strategies. I would regularly hear comments such as, "There's no reason why we can't do this." Leaders were invigorated and energized by the process and embraced the new context they were working in, evaluating the external conditions and also looking internally at the organization to critically assess their own skills and the capabilities of the organization.

NEW KNOWLEDGE

A sense of new knowledge came from what was learned from the process. Much like their surfer counterparts, these leaders were catching a wave of new ideas. Companies were more focused and consistent with their efforts because they now had a process-driven approach to overcoming new challenges. The companies that found success as a result of going through this process were able to generate new strategies to overcome challenges they had not attempted before. The companies not willing to embark on this new journey continued to flounder in the new conditions, barely making it off shore, fighting mental battles with themselves or others, and resisting any kind of real change. The pressing needs of the day-to-day prevented them from seeing the big picture of what the process could produce. There was a noticeable difference between the companies that stuck with the status quo and those that departed from the norm and embraced the principles of the surfer.

3. IMPORTANCE OF THE PRINCIPLES

NEW PROCESS

The principles are important because we need a new process for success. We are struggling in the new conditions with old tactics and strategies, wondering why our efforts have failed or didn't go according to plan. At the same time, there's pressure to invest in new technology platforms, software, and social media without organizations having a real understanding of their true benefit. The Ride the Wave Process provides clarity around market challenges and uses a new set of principles that will help make organizations successful in the new conditions. The process reevaluates changing market conditions, aligns internal skills with the discovered market challenges, and encourages exploration of new strategies through testing, prototyping, and learning from mistakes. Framing the process around surfing helps make the strategic planning process new, motivating, and fun.

NEW INNOVATION

The principles will help business leaders uncover new ways to innovate and develop new solutions to traditional problems. The process pulls leaders out from under the weight of the status quo and creates a new perspective that is more consistent with the business conditions they are working in. The process also forces leadership to think differently and more critically about the strategic changes that need to be made. The principles are used to look both externally at the market conditions and then internally at the organization to provide a holistic process for building skills in the market. Many of the traditional processes, models, and methods do not take a holistic look at the external challenges or the current skills inside an organization. Innovation occurs when an honest assessment of both the external and internal is used to create new strategies and a new way to think about success.

NEW SUCCESS

Ride the Wave is a process that helps organizations to reframe success. A new approach to risk is the starting point for finding success in the new conditions. The surfer exemplifies the new approach and how to use risk exploration to find success. For surfers, it's a steady progression of building new skills and smaller accomplishments over time. Companies that embrace this new approach by using the principles will embrace a new way to think about and find success. They can use incremental changes as a way to progress successfully over time, thinking about success over a series of progressive moves toward a new initiative instead of betting the house on short-term gambles that can be hit or miss. Companies can find success by thinking about their efforts as building toward future success and not trying to force it in the short term.

THE PRINCIPLES

1. EMBRACE THE CONDITIONS

GET IN THE WATER

In understanding the three principles, it's important to provide some context around the sport of surfing. Surfing is one of the most popular and progressive sports in the world. The single most important factor in surfing is the conditions and the waves. Surfers get in the water and put themselves in the conditions to catch some waves. Surf reports and forecasts help to give surfers insight into what the ocean might hold for them on a given day, but the timing of waves is an unknown, and catching them at the right time means that you need to be in the water to do so. Surfers embrace the uncertainty of not knowing exactly when a wave will break, but put themselves into the unknown conditions in order to catch one. Surfers have faith that at some point a wave will roll in, so embracing the conditions is the first step to making that happen.

GET IN THE LINE-UP

After getting in the water, surfers must be in the right position to catch a wave. That place in the ocean where surfers wait for waves is called the line-up. Surfers form a "line" in the water

THREE PRINCIPLES OF THE SURFER

and will take turns paddling into waves. Being in the line-up and in the correct position for an incoming wave is critical. If you're in the wrong place at the wrong time, you could miss a wave or get caught in the impact zone of a breaking wave that could come crashing down on your head. In addition to the breaking waves, you're also contending with other surfers in the line-up. You might be in a line-up with locals who have been surfing that spot for years. Localism is an intimidating part of surfing and can cause you to miss waves or even physical pain if you're not respecting or acknowledging the local surfers. If you disrespect the line-up or act like a "kook," expect a verbal tongue-lashing or physical beat down that could put you out of the line-up and out of commission.

GET ON A WAVE

After you have braved the conditions and put yourself in the line-up, you're now ready to catch a wave. Waves are strong, powerful, and unpredictable. They build natural momentum miles out in the ocean and then make their way toward shore, traveling a great distance to break on reef formations under the water and causing them to release all that energy as they come crashing toward the shore. Waves will "pitch" up or come out of the water as they move toward shore. As they pitch, waves start to "break" either straight over the top or to the right or the left. Knowing how a wave will break or knowing which direction it will break determines how a surfer will catch a wave. A wave will also barrel and create a steep slope with a small pocket for a surfer to ride as it breaks into shore. Understanding the conditions and how each unique wave will break is critical. Knowing where to be in the water and what the wave will do once it breaks is important, but you will also need a unique set of skills if you plan to ride it successfully.

2. PROGRESSION-BASED MINDSET

BUILD YOUR SKILLS

Once the surfer understands the conditions and is in position to catch a wave, having the ability to paddle into a wave and catch it is the next set of skills needed. However, this is much harder than it sounds and being able to take what you now know about the conditions and apply it to surfing is more of an art than a science. Mastering the basics of a pop-up and standing up on the board is a large part of what's needed to catch a wave. But surfing with style and progression is what separates the beginner from the pro. Surfers use progression to describe moving through a set of tricks or learning a new skill on their boards. Progression is so ingrained into the sport that any comparison between two surfers is based on progression. It's also used to describe the sport as a whole and how the sport is "progressing" in terms of tricks, wave size, and technical ability. Surfers that understand progression know that it's the key to building any new skill. Without progression, surfers would not move forward and would remain static in their skills. Progression is about being adaptable to the conditions and having the mindset not to settle for the status quo.

CHANGE YOUR MINDSET

The mindset needed for progression in surfing is focused on action toward learning something new. A surfer's mindset is focused on adding a new trick to their repertoire and building upon their previous accomplishments. Progression, then, is about learning from and using those accomplishments as a starting point for doing something new. The mindset of a surfer is focused on movement or progress. "Progression-based mindsets" are what surfers use to describe someone who is committed to building new surf skills. It also reflects the mindset of someone who is determined to accomplish a goal. Forward movement that is progressive builds on previous success and reflects a mindset committed to change. In order to successfully build your skills as a surfer in the ocean or a business professional in the new conditions, you will need to adopt a progression-based mindset toward new skills.

FIND THE CALM

As skills are being built with a mindset focused on progression, surfers enter a type of zone or a calm where they react and execute rather than think about what they're doing. After hours of practice and execution, surfers will see consistency in their riding and naturally improve their trick progression without thinking about it. Surfers don't need to think about what they are doing. Instead, they use their training and react to the changing conditions. Pattern recognition and instincts take over, and actions become instinctive rather than planned or managed. Surfers often describe a "flow state" where they are physically committed and mentally focused on the task at hand and not anything else. Surfers can then react to whatever is thrown in their way and feel the sensation or "stoke" as a result of the culmination of preparation, practice, and that sense of accomplishment when everything comes together on a single wave.

3. RISK AS A COMPASS

RISK EXPOSURE

As laid-back as surfers are, there is an aggressive side to their sport that is important to understand as well. Surfers take on risk when riding waves and use that aggressive approach to feed their trick progression and style, building skills and exposing themselves to risks that are more severe than in any other sport out there. Surfers use risk as a compass that points them in the right direction, and they practice a controlled method of risk exposure in order to progress at what they do. Surfers in the ocean, regardless of skill or ability, willingly expose themselves to new risk every time they paddle out on their boards. There are risks that come from attempting new tricks and risks from the conditions that are within the ocean. The ocean can cause the surfer harm if they are not mindful of the conditions and risks that are always there. The risk exposure continues to increase every time a surfer decides to do something new.

CONSEQUENCES OF RISK

With exposure to risk come consequences. As a surfer, if you are not managing the conditions and do not have the skills to catch a wave or the mindset to progress and improve, you will face the consequences of your actions. The conditions can change and spiral out of control if not managed properly. The unknown or unpredictable risks can catch even the best surfers in the world off guard. Surfers can get "caught inside" or within the "impact zone" of where the waves are breaking. This can happen when a surfer is paddling out through a set of waves and doesn't make it to the line-up or when a surfer takes a wipeout, gets caught in the impact zone, and is unable to get back to the board and out of danger. This can also happen when a set of large waves comes through and creates what's called a "clean up set." This can physically take out the entire line-up and "clean up" everything in its path. All of these are examples of the consequences of risks that surfers face when embracing the conditions and trying to progress by building new skills.

RESULTS OF RISK

After a surfer manages the consequences, the level of risk continues to rise as surfers take on bigger waves and attempt new tricks. Surfers who want to improve and use risk to progress will all experience wipeouts, slams, and bails if they want to progress. Wiping out on a wave presents another set of hidden risks that are buried just below the surface.

Reefs, fish, and plants all become potential risks to the surfer underwater. You're now at the mercy of the ocean and the elements in the depths below. Surfers can get pushed down to the very bottom of the ocean floor, among the reefs and rocks below. The conditions can be unforgiving, and the waves are relentless. There are no do-overs. You can't press pause, and you can't have a second chance once you've committed to your wave and the risks that come with it.

THREE PRINCIPLES TO PROCESS

1. EXPECTATIONS

INITIATION

After gaining some insight into surfing and the background of the principles, here's what to expect as you begin to learn more about how to use these principles as a process. Just like the surfers who paddle out into unknown conditions, focus their mindset toward progression, and use risk to point them toward new challenges, you will face new obstacles as you begin using this process. The first challenge will be the initiation of the process and just getting started. For some people, this will be the toughest part. Anything new takes time to understand and even longer to implement. However, the three principles are meant to give you a simple and easy process for overcoming any new challenge. Just like the surfer, you will need to be in the water to get started and understand the principles. The process will only begin after an initiation and once the principles are put into practice.

THE ROAD OF TRIALS

As you begin to use the process and take a hard look at your individual skills and organizational capabilities, you will intentionally try to avoid this new change because of the risks involved. Whenever you can and wherever possible, avoid trying to protect yourself and be open to these new risks. This process will be hard and almost counterintuitive to what you've done in the past. But just like the surfer, you will want to change your mindset about your skills and take on risk in order to improve. This might mean failing to execute a new marketing or sales strategy or struggling with something new that was outside your comfort zone. This is okay, but you will need to be disciplined and work hard to solve these internal struggles. As you use the principles and this new process, you will go down the road less traveled. There will be trials and tests along the way. Remember that this is a process and that the principles are a guide to take you on a journey to somewhere new. The road will no longer be paved, but will now be bumpy, full of obstacles, and give you a few scars along the way.

ALLIES AND ENEMIES

Along the road of trials, you will find that your actions will either garner allies or enemies. People will either be 100 percent supportive of your efforts to do something new or they will potentially become an obstacle in your way. More often than not, you will find that colleagues will support you and will even go out of their way to help you accomplish what you have set out to do. If you are passionate, prepared, and have positioned the new initiative in a way that people can support, you will have people who will get behind you. Unfortunately, there will also be people who stand in your way. It's just human nature. There will be people who see your efforts to create change as a threat to their way of doing things. It's human nature to protect one's self, so if you are pushing an agenda of change that might be good for you and the organization, there's a good chance that others might undermine your efforts. The principles and the process will help you to eliminate those kinds of professional obstacles and build support among allies—not enemies.

2. CONSIDERATIONS

CHALLENGES

As you use the three principles, you will be tested repeatedly and will need to overcome various challenges along the way. There are considerations you will need to make in using the process and how your organization will make changes. You will obviously want to avoid challenges that cause harm as a result of your actions, but you need to be open to failure if you are going to do anything new and bold. The challenges you will face will cause you to question your actions and the decisions you will need to make. It will be easier to abandon your decision or stray from the journey since the processes within your organization will support the old way of doing things. Your challenge will be to persevere in the face of these new challenges, and when it becomes difficult or hard, remember that this is a process and that the long-term benefits outweigh the short-term trade-offs.

TEMPTATION

The temptation will be to go back to the old way of doing things. It's harder to take a new path than it is to slip back into old habits, so using the new process will be hard. The temptation to revert back to the old way, even if it doesn't produce new or better results, will be favorable to anything with a perceived high level of risk. You will need to avoid these temptations, overcome the new challenges, and know that exploring the risks will be important to the overall process as you begin to ride the wave. Again, it might be colleagues or even customers that will push you back in the direction of the old way of doing things. Establishing milestones and check-ins will be important, but so will having a long-term view, which will help you to avoid temptations that are comfortable or easy.

MASTERY

The process will give you a sense of control and a better understanding of how you can improve at what you're doing. Organizations and leadership that are struggling often complain about not having control or not having a sense of control. A big part of the Ride the Wave Process is about regaining that sense of control—gaining control through new knowledge but also through understanding that this is a process and that you will need patience on the journey. The process shows results over time, and like anything in life that is new, it's important to think about the process as a path to mastery. While on the path, it's important to work through the process and develop new skills or capabilities over time, mastering them the longer you travel along the path. The process helps you to take a long-term approach to developing new skills and capabilities as well as solving short-term challenges that present themselves.

3. MANAGEMENT

SERIES OF TESTS

As you go through the process, you will encounter a series of tests for you and your organization. Successfully managing each of these tests will be as important as implementing the new marketing or sales initiative itself. Creating a new context around your initiatives will be important for the organization, and having accountability measures in place for your teams will help to support the successful execution of your new plans. These tests are more manageable when the initiatives are supported by the entire organization and reinforced through company-wide training and development programs. Each part of the process will encourage you to take new action, and having a management process to support the organization during each of the tests will give you a better chance of success. The process will ensure that new initiatives stick around and do not become another failed project that had a lot of steam and momentum up front, but was beat down over time by new obstacles that tested the organization.

CATCHING WAVES

Throughout the process, there will be new challenges that will be hard to overcome. Anything new is difficult and the new conditions will be in opposition to what you're trying to do. That feeling of "catching waves" is what will keep you on the path, moving you toward the next obstacle. Just like the surfer who encounters bigger and more challenging waves, as a business leader, you will have to take on new and increasingly difficult market challenges. The challenges, like waves, will become more difficult as you create more and more change within your organization. Your new mindset will force you to take on these challenges and to develop the new skills to overcome them. The risk will increase the more you push yourself and the organization through the process. As your skills develop, you will conquer bigger and more challenging "waves." Your new role as a big wave surfer will be to challenge the status quo and face greater risk versus trying to avoid it and play it safe.

THE AGONY AND THE ECSTASY

While you are riding the wave and overcoming greater and greater challenges, you will have moments of ecstasy where things will feel like they're working and that you are building momentum. These moments are important to acknowledge and celebrate. They will provide you with a sense of progress and accomplishment. The process will frame these accomplishments as small steps along a much a longer path. You will be satisfied with what you've done but will still want more. The surfer catches a wave, rides in the barrel, and feels the stoke from the accomplishment. Once the surfer completes the ride, it doesn't stop there. The mindset of the surfer is to do it again and recreate that moment. There will also be moments of agony that you will encounter, but that sense of moving the needle forward and accomplishing something new will keep you pushing beyond the small setbacks. Just avoiding complacency and knowing that the process of riding the wave is preparing you for the next opportunity will put you in a position to capitalize on it.

SECTION III:
BE MORE LIKE THE SURFER

"To convince people to back your idea, you've got to sell it to yourself and know when it's the moment. Sometimes that means waiting. It's like surfing. You don't create energy, you just harvest energy already out there."

—James Cameron

PRINCIPLE I: EMBRACE THE CONDITIONS

7

SURFERS EMBRACE THE CONDITIONS

1. THE CONDITIONS

IMPORTANCE OF CONDITIONS

After becoming more familiar with the three principles and learning some of the background around surfing, let's take a closer look at how each of the principles can serve as a guide for what we need to do differently in the new conditions. The first principle is to Embrace the Conditions. The conditions are important for surfers because they can dictate the level of success that a surfer can have. Surfers are always evaluating the conditions, trying to figure out whether or not there will be surf. Good conditions can bring exhilaration, but poor conditions can bring frustration and disappointment and also leave surfers feeling dissatisfied. Surfers put themselves in a position to surf regardless of the conditions. They train, prepare, and wait for hours for the opportunity to catch a single wave, but their patience is rewarded when they do catch one and experience that moment of exhilaration because they have embraced it.

SURFERS AND CONDITIONS

For the surfer, part of embracing the conditions is about having patience. They know that waves will come, but also that waiting for the right opportunity is part of the process. Surfers watch the horizon for the next approaching wave and put themselves in a position to catch it. The surfer will need to manage conditions that include rogue waves, rip currents, plant life, and sea life like sharks and jellyfish. Surfers are constantly scanning for opportunities to catch waves but also balancing the risks against the changing conditions in the ocean. Surfers are focused on catching waves for themselves, but still work cooperatively to help identify waves that might cause harm to others—or even threats from the occasional "kook" who is new to surfing and could injure another surfer with a stray board or an overly aggressive attempt on a tough wave. Managing the ever-changing conditions is the first thing that surfers need to do and the first principle to achieving success in their sport.

EMBRACE THE CONDITIONS

The idea of embracing the conditions is important to surfing because more often than not, the conditions will not be ideal. There might not be waves, there might be too many surfers, or the weather might make a session more challenging than it needs to be. Surfers embrace what's happening in the water and accept the conditions they are given. Surfers who embrace the conditions know that eventually the conditions will improve. A wave will come in, the sun will come out, and the crowds will die down. When surfers embrace the conditions, it's important for them to have the right mindset. They stay patient and hungry, keeping their minds calm but aware. They have an inner focus about what is happening around them, using the information presented and evaluating the challenges as well as the opportunities.

2. SURFERS AND CONDITIONS

SURF REPORTS

Just like in business, surfing has been disrupted by new technology, and surfers use new platforms to analyze information about the conditions. Now, more than ever before, surfers are using technology to manage the conditions and find the best opportunities to catch waves. Even with satellites and weather reports to monitor the conditions, surfers can't predict the exact moment a wave will break. Surfers can track weather patterns and know when the swell might come their way. Just like in business, however, predicting the exact moment a sale might happen is virtually impossible to do. Surfers use the new technology in reporting to identify opportunities and embrace the conditions by being out there and being ready for them. There is no guarantee that a wave will break, but reports provide enough information to surfers and point them to the right conditions to catch a wave.

TRAVEL

Because of this new technology and hyperaccurate surf reports, surfers can find information online via websites such as surfline.com to determine where waves will be breaking. There are also oceanographers that track surf activity and report on what is taking place at the best surf spots around the world. This technology creates opportunities for the surfer to monitor conditions and determine where the surf will be next. Instead of spending days and hours waiting at surf spots that may never produce a wave, surfers can now travel around the world to surf breaks where waves are being predicted. Surfers can easily travel to these spots, cut out the downtime between surf sessions, and experience a fresh set of waves anywhere around the world.

TIME

Surfers are now able to travel from surf break to surf break and create more opportunities to surf, which decreases the downtime between catching waves. A professional surfer can be in California one day and then in Australia the next after predicting the conditions through real-time reporting. Instead of being tied to a specific surf spot and forced to wait for the next set of waves, surfers can anticipate where the surf might be next and be there when it breaks. Like snowboarders looking for fresh powder, surfers can use a combination of weather reporting and ocean technology to manage the conditions, evaluate their opportunities, and be in a position to catch guaranteed waves. As surfers continue to use technology to evaluate the conditions, they increase the likelihood of finding success and catching waves.

3. MICK FANNING

MICK AND CONDITIONS

Part of embracing the conditions is using the latest in technology and information-sharing platforms to identify opportunities to surf waves. Another part of embracing the conditions is simply getting out there and being in the ocean. For beginners, this can be the hardest and most challenging part of surfing. Of all the challenging conditions a surfer can encounter, dealing with ocean predators is the most publicized aspect of the sport. It's also the one obstacle in surfing that brings out the most fear in people because of the movie *Jaws* and the media firestorm every time there's an attack. Sharks are the most feared predator in the ocean, and based on the attention they receive, you would think that shark attacks happen on a regular basis. But the truth is that they happen very rarely, and you actually have a better chance of a lot of other things happening to you before a shark decides to come after you. That fear of sharks has never fazed surfer Mick Fanning, and if anyone would have an excuse not to embrace the conditions, it would be him.

SHARK ATTACK

In August of 2015, Mick was participating in a surf contest in South Africa. Jeffreys Bay is east of Port Elizabeth, and the J-Bay Open is a regular stop on the world surf tour. The event is televised on live TV and attended by some of the biggest names in surfing. At the time, Fanning was ranked number four in the world, was a previous triple-crown winner, and was competing against Julian Wilson in the finals of the contest. Mick was waiting for a wave when the cameras captured a large fin in the water behind him. A shark made a large splash behind Fanning. Mick turned to defend himself from the predator, and with cameras still on him, a large wave blocked the view of what was happening. The TV announcers thought Mick had been taken under. Contest organizers sent in rescue boats and jet skis to pull Fanning from the water. Mick escaped unharmed, but the contest was called off because of the incident. When reliving the incident safely onshore, Fanning said, "I'm happy to not even compete ever again. Seriously, to walk away from that, I'm just so stoked."

TOUR WIN

The next year, Fanning returned to J-Bay to compete in the same contest where he had escaped the shark attack. For the twelve months leading up to the contest, he had surfed a reduced schedule and only competed in a few contests. The attack had taken its toll. Fanning was hesitant to get back in the water after such a dramatic experience but decided he needed to in order to compete. Mick did not want what happened to prevent him from competing in the event or from ever surfing again. Fanning not only competed, but he also made it to the finals to surf for the title. He won the event in a dramatic fashion and overcame his fear of getting back into the water. "That was always the intention, to come back—to right the wrongs of last year," he said. "Now we have, we can move on." Mick is the example of what it means to embrace the conditions—not allowing the conditions to dictate failure or success, but embracing the challenges and turning them into opportunities for success.

NEW BUSINESS CONDITIONS

1. NEW DECISION JOURNEY

NEW PLATFORMS

Just as there are ever-changing conditions within the ocean for surfers, there are also changing market conditions for business leaders. The biggest change is the dominance of customers and how they have been able to gain more control within the buying process. Their needs and wants have become more transparent as well as more important to the marketing and sales process. It has become more challenging than ever to grab the attention of customers and to hold onto it. With the advent of new information-sharing platforms and the use of mobile devices at their fingertips, buyers are able to find information faster and have used that information to leverage buying power with organizations. These new platforms have increased the expectations of consumers, and their behavior has become more social and real-time. Customers now use multiple channels to make a purchase decision on a product or service.

NEW INFORMATION

The advent of technology has brought customers and companies closer to together, but customers have access to more information-sharing platforms, and the purchase power has shifted from organizations to the consumer. The demand for transparency and having their needs met has become a priority for customers, and they know about your product before they even contact your organization. Even though companies are closer to the customer, there is still a gap with how best to connect with them and impact the buying process. Customers have a wealth of information about who you are and what you do, leaving little to no control over the narrative about a product or service. Organizations are struggling to participate in a process that is happening independent of their efforts and the conversations that are created within the consumer market.

NEW BUYING PROCESS

It's estimated that most customers are more than 75 percent of the way along a decision journey before they connect with someone from an organization about a product or service. This means that consumers want to experience a product or service for themselves before they interact with someone from your organization. This dynamic can put companies and leadership in a position of having less influence on the customer buying process. When left to customers or the market, your organization becomes defined by those perceptions and in what is being said. If you're not telling your story, the story of your product or service is told for you. The new skill for management is the ability to identify, adapt to, and understand this new buying process. Organizations that do not change or adapt could miss opportunities to meet the needs of an ever-changing market.

2. THE STATUS QUO

DON'T USE TECHNOLOGY

Companies that adhere to the status quo and do not embrace the new conditions are not using or leveraging new technology or information-sharing platforms. These companies are not "in the water," either because they don't understand or don't know how to use the new platforms. Some organizations are not using CRM and marketing automation platforms or not leveraging social media because they don't think it's needed or relevant to their business. They have gone without it for so long that they think they can continue to survive by sticking with what has brought them success in the past. The problem is that new technology is so prevalent within all industries and markets that every organization, regardless of the industry, is using some form of new technology within their business. Every kind of organization, from those that are service-based to manufacturing, will need to embrace the new platforms available, not only to compete but also to stay ahead of competition. Any organization can benefit from new technology—those that don't suffer at their own peril.

DON'T UNDERSTAND BUYERS

Organizations that are struggling in the new conditions don't understand the new buying behavior of their customers and don't know their unique decision journey. Within the new market conditions, there has been a shift in the dynamic between customers and organizations. No longer is the organization in the driver's seat, steering the marketing to sales process. Customers and consumers are now able to use information-sharing platforms to learn about products and services. Consumers are buying products and services in a new way and keeping the organization out of the process until later, after they have made their decision. In the past, organizations pushed customers through a traditional funnel process to make a purchase decision, but because of the new conditions, customers are able to jump in at any point in the buying process. They find the information specific to their needs and manage the process on their own or on a separate path from marketing or sales professionals.

DON'T EVALUATE CONDITIONS

Organizations that do not embrace the conditions will never overcome the challenges in markets because they're not evaluating what's changing. They are overly focused internally on the organization and do not scan the external conditions to see how customers are making purchase decisions. They are so focused on keeping up with competition that they don't attempt to lead in their respective markets. Most organizations evaluate the external conditions based on a perception of themselves in the market versus how the customer actually sees them. Customer problems are fluid and always changing. The way we live and work is also changing—as are the problems and challenges for customers. We all have less time but more choice in terms of how we solve those problems. If an organization is not keeping up with the changes, the company will not evolve with the market and will struggle to embrace the new conditions.

3. THE RESULTS

DON'T EVOLVE

Organizations that maintain the status quo, don't change their approach, and don't embrace the new conditions all experience the same poor results. When they do not explore new technology or look for new ways to improve systems and processes, they do not evolve. However, the organizations that are evolving in the new conditions are using software and automation wherever possible. Marketing to sales systems are being automated from beginning to end in order to speed up lead profiling and qualifications and pass this information to sales professionals in the field. Organizations are evolving by taking the human factor out of processes to improve internal systems and can now provide real-time responses to customer requests. If you're competing with an organization that is leveraging these kinds of technologies, and you are not, you will be blown away by your competition. You will not be evolving to meet the needs of customers that prefer to buy this way in these new conditions and not evolving with the market changes, which will slowly erode your competitive advantage. Customers will find alternatives to your product or service.

DON'T CHANGE

When organizations are not exploring buyer behavior and do not understand the new way that customers buy, they continue to solve problems the way they did years ago and don't change. As customers become savvier about how they find information and make decisions about products or services, organizations will need to change to meet the customers' new level of expertise. Consumers have never had so much information at their fingertips or so much choice when it comes to products or services. Smaller, more nimble companies that can unbundle services and become experts at a specific niche are now challenging larger organizations that have been around for years. Banks are no longer the only type of organization that can provide payment services. Companies such as PayPal and Square are helping organizations collect money from customers and making it easier, less of a hassle, and also cheaper. If companies do not evolve to meet how customers now want to buy products or services, they will lose out to the smaller, more progressive companies that do.

DON'T EVALUATE

When organizations do not embrace the conditions and evaluate them on a consistent basis, they lose the ability to manage the changes. Embracing the conditions is about understanding the market and making incremental changes on a regular basis to adapt to what is happening. Knowing that you are in the conditions and in a position to catch the next wave of success or avoid the next disaster is key.

Embracing the conditions is about anticipating what's next in the short term, but also about evaluating the conditions and planning for what's next in the long term. Organizations that are not scanning markets or evaluating their position against competition can lose their ability to stay relevant or even effective in the market. Embracing and consistently evaluating the conditions are important and key to finding success when using the first principle.

THE NEW PRINCIPLE

1. HOW TO EMBRACE THE CONDITIONS

MAP THE JOURNEY

Just like the surfer who paddles out into the water over and over again, business leaders will have to embrace these new market conditions and adapt accordingly. One of the first things to understand about the new conditions is that there is a new customer decision journey and that the traditional marketing to sales approach has changed. No longer is there a linear marketing to sales process or a funnel where customers all enter at the same point and work their way to a purchase decision. The funnel has been replaced with a circular process where customers can access stages on their own, independent of your organization. The first step that business leaders can take is to chart the customer journey by identifying touch-points and customer needs at each of those stages. Figuring out each step in the customer's unique decision journey and the stages where you are either meeting those needs or falling short will be vital.

MEASURE YOUR ACTIONS

Measure your actions by using tools and technology after you have mapped out the customer's decision journey. The new technology that is disrupting markets can also be used to work in your favor. Use technology to make better decisions, streamline systems or processes, and help measure your results against the actions you are taking. There is a wealth of data that leadership can use to measure and manage the customer decision journey. Leaders can create compelling content to attract customers and enhance their knowledge or experience with products or services, but also to measure which are most effective. Through these interactions, you will be able to create a compelling narrative and also assess what is working and what is not. Integrate organizational structures to focus on sales and marketing collaboration, but use the latest in technology to make this process easy. The new customer decision journey requires sales and marketing to work together at each stage of the process to meet customer needs. You need to have a seamless and integrated process to help you embrace the new conditions, but also to measure the results.

CREATE A PROCESS

Once you have mapped out the customer journey and are using technology to measure your performance, create a repeatable process that can be evaluated on a regular basis. Organizations will need to create a repeatable process for evaluating the customer decision journey and where they are having success along it. Once you have an established process and know where you are having success, you can start to allocate your resources accordingly. When you map the journeys and find points where your tactics are successful, you can reallocate sales and marketing resources to the activities that are most likely to influence a purchase decision. You can also pull resources from initiatives that are not making an impact. Track customer decision journeys, reallocate resources along the path, and test your assumptions. There is no need to wait for the perfect market conditions. The market conditions will always be changing and a repeatable process will help you to evolve right along with them.

2. THE BENEFIT

THE DECISION JOURNEY

Like the surfer, the organizations that find success all start by embracing the conditions and then make changes to the organization that match the customer's decision journey. When organizations map out the customer decision journey for their product or service, they can create sales and marketing efficiencies, save the organization money by reallocating resources to more effective strategies, and decrease the length of the overall sales cycle. Companies willing to adapt to the new conditions and take a more progressive approach to using technology platforms will also have better success than those that do not. Organizations that are willing to take a chance on a new strategy or tactic are more likely to meet the needs of the customer at the different points along their decision journey. They are also more likely to use new digital tools and technology more fully, allocate sales and marketing resources more effectively, and create collaboration efforts across the organization.

THE BENEFIT

When organizations map out the customer decision journey, they can gain a 20 percent increase in customer leads, 10 percent growth in first-time customers, and 20 percent increase in the speed to qualifying a lead and closing a deal.[1] These

1 Oskar Lingqvist, Candace Lun Plotkin, and Jennifer Stanley, "Do You Really Understand How Your Business Customers Buy?" *McKinsey Quarterly*, February 2015, http://www.mckinsey.com/business-functions/marketing-and-sales/our-

results can benefit any organization that wants to improve how they market and sell products or services, but the challenge becomes dedicating the time to explore this journey from the customer's perspective and then taking the steps to implement the process fully. Most organizations have not taken the time to explore the decision journey of their customer and are still too focused internally on the organization to understand the significance of this change in the conditions. Leaders within organizations who know and understand how their customers buy have succeeded where others have failed.

THE RESULT

Companies that are successful year after year all use the first principle of embracing the conditions. These organizations map out how the customer makes a purchase decision to buy their product or service. They also measure what customers do on their site, have a good understanding of who visits them, and know the best way to follow up with the potential customer. After they have determined the unique journey for the customer and measured their success, they are better able to allocate resources accordingly. For example, a real estate firm can manage every step of the process from the point when a customer visits their site, fills out a buyer or seller contact form, and even how their firm will reach back out to make contact with that potential client. The firm can then match the expectations of the buyer or seller with skills and abilities of one of their agents and have established practices in place to move someone from making a simple inquiry online to making a purchase decision on a property. The company can map the journey, create a repeatable process, and support the buyer's needs when they embrace the new conditions.

---

insights/do-you-really-understand-how-your-business-customers-buy.

3. MY JOURNEY

NEW CAR

One of the biggest changes within retail is the new way that customers buy and how marketing and sales organizations have had to change how they approach offering products and services. The power dynamic has flipped, with customers now demanding more transparency and wanting a simpler way to make purchase decisions. The auto industry has experienced this change more so than any other industry and has changed its approach to marketing and sales considerably. The way consumers buy both new and used cars is drastically different than the way it was even just a few years ago. I experienced this firsthand from the customer's perspective when I made my first ever car purchase in the summer of 2014. My first ever car was a graduation gift from my parents that they gave me after graduation from college so I could drive myself to work. After a few months, however, I landed a new job that included a company car, so I sold my first car to pay down student loans.

DECISION JOURNEY

For the next fifteen years, I would own a number of different fleet cars and never actually had to go through the process of buying a new car for myself. When it came to buying my first car, I researched cars online to determine what my new car would be. Living in a city, I knew I would be making short trips, parking at meters, and that I would not spend much time on freeways. I would never have to haul anything more than a few bags of groceries in the backseat. In doing my research, I looked at new, small, and Italian cars. I quickly discovered Fiat and thought that a small, black Italian car at the right price would be more car than I would ever need. During my process, I scoured the Fiat website, read online reviews, watched videos, and talked to my friends about Fiats as well. In the span of a few days, I had all the information I needed and was ready to connect with my local Fiat dealership to make a purchase.

DEALERSHIP AS CONCIERGE

I emailed a sales representative at a local dealership about the kind of Fiat I was looking for. I sent a list of cars that I was interested in and gave specific details about what I wanted, including colors, seat materials, stereo preferences, and I even requested red brake calipers with mag wheels. Within a few minutes, the sales representative had used my list to find a similar car at another local dealership and asked if I wanted to see the car that afternoon. After viewing the car in the parking lot with Kate, sitting in the leather seats, and kicking the tires a bit, I said to the salesperson, "Looks great. Let's do this." My statement was met with a startled look from Kate, who informed me that a test drive was actually the next step in the process. But feeling confident in the work I had done to come to this decision, I responded, "This is actually exactly the car I want, and I'm not sure a test drive will change my mind." After that, I did some paperwork and then took home my Italian beauty after just a few days of research and decision-making. This process illustrates how consumers, like myself, now buy and how there's a new journey for customers in the new conditions.

PRINCIPLE II: ADOPT A PROGRESSION- BASED MINDSET

8

MINDSET OF SURFERS

1. PROGRESSION-BASED

CONCEPT OF PROGRESSION

The second principle is to adopt a Progression-Based Mindset toward individual skills and organizational capabilities. Business leaders have a lot to learn from the mindset of the surfer. Understanding how surfers view progression is important since it's one of the fundamental concepts within their sport. Progression can be defined as forward movement or "progressing" toward something new by making gradual improvements in your abilities and becoming better at what you do. A progression-based mindset is what surfers use to develop their skills and abilities. Surfing is an individual sport, and surfers use progression to push themselves to do more tricks, improve their style, and get better at their sport. Surfers measure and compare themselves to one another in terms of their progression. How a surfer is progressing is the universal way that surfers build new skills and capabilities in comparison to one another. It also refers to how the sport of surfing is progressing as a whole or what surfers are doing to progressively change it.

PROGRESSION IN PRACTICE

Surfers at any level have a mindset based on progression and forward movement toward new skills. They are always trying to get better at their sport, regardless of their current skills or abilities. All surfers approach their sport from the standpoint of progression, meaning they are always looking to improve upon what they did previously. This mindset is very different from other sports and radically different from the way most business leaders approach their professional roles. Surfers go out for a session, catch waves, and incrementally try to improve upon what they did each time they ride. Surfers will try to ride a wave longer, try a new cutback or to ride the lip of the wave, and even perform an aerial maneuver. There is an unlimited number of ways to progress a simple trick or move it forward. Tricks can be done forward, backward, regular-foot, goofy-foot, switch, frontside, backside, and the list goes on and on. These technical terms are specific to surfing and show that there is always something new that can be done.

PROGRESSION AS A MINDSET

Imagine yourself as the surfer, standing on the beach and thinking about what you will do that is new every time you head out into the ocean. Try to put yourself in the place of a surfer and really embrace the mindset of continuously adding new skills. It's daunting even to consider how hard this would be in the business world, but surfers not only have to think about what they are already able to do, but also what they need to accomplish next. Progression is about having the mindset and confidence in what you already know, but also about having the motivation or inner drive to do something different than you did before. Progression is not just applied to skills and abilities since surfers also use it to develop new equipment and develop their wave knowledge as well.

2. SURFERS AND PROGRESSION

TECHNOLOGY

In addition to skills and abilities, there are other areas within surfing where progression has made an impact. Each area has progressed the sport of surfing to where it is today, but can also provide insight into ways that marketing and sales professionals could approach new business strategies using progression. The first area is technology and how new platforms have helped to progress the sport by providing surfers with more information about waves and surf conditions. Instead of playing a guessing game and trying to figure out when and where waves might break, surfers are able to use sites such as surfline.com and forecasting models to predict the whims of the waves. Swell reports and forecasting have become more reliable and more accessible to the surfing masses. Surfline.com is now the go-to source for surf conditions around the world, and a single visit to the site will provide you with a report on the surf as well as cameras that allow you to view the waves in real time.

EQUIPMENT

The progression of equipment has allowed surfers to ride bigger waves and in more challenging conditions. During the birth of surfing, Polynesians that settled in Hawaii used heavy wood boards to ride waves back to shore after fishing. The sport has obviously progressed from a mode of ocean transportation to a recreational sport, and the materials used have changed significantly as well. No longer are boards made of heavy wood, but of Styrofoam and fiberglass that is lighter and more buoyant in the water. The lighter material has also allowed surfers to progress the types of maneuvers they do on their boards. Since the boards are lighter, surfers are able to do more cutbacks, aerials, and lip maneuvers that were never imagined or conceived of on the heavier wood boards years ago. Surfers also added fins that provide more control, leashes that provide an element of safety while in the water, and wetsuits that protect surfers from the cold water temperatures and harsh ocean conditions, such as reefs, plants, and sea life.

WAVE KNOWLEDGE

As the technology for predicting waves has improved alongside the equipment, surfers have been able to find and ride bigger and better waves. Technology has progressed surfing toward bigger waves, and the equipment has helped surfers to ride them. As the sport has progressed in terms of technology, equipment, and skills, so has the size of the waves that surfers are now able to ride. In recent years, surfers have pushed toward surfing bigger and bigger waves, with pro Laird Hamilton being seen as the big wave pioneer within the sport. The limiting factor has always been the knowledge of big waves and the equipment used to ride them. With technology enhancements continually affecting equipment, surfers continue to progress toward surfing bigger and more dangerous waves. They have improved their understanding of larger waves and the equipment needed to ride them. As the waves get bigger, the stakes are higher, and the need for new technology and equipment only pushes the progression of the sport further.

3. KELLY SLATER

KELLY AND PROGRESSION

When looking to identify with someone in surfing who exemplifies progression in the sport, the obvious choice is Kelly Slater. Slater is the Derek Jeter of surfing, and at forty-four, he is also one of the veterans of the sport, still competing in and winning contests on a regular basis. Slater has won the ASP World Tour a record eleven times over a twenty-five-year span between when he won his first title in 1992 and his final year of competition and planned retirement after the 2017 season. Kelly still competes at the highest level within surfing while being one of the oldest competitors in the sport. Over the years, Slater has remained relevant and progressed in the sport by consistently developing his skills and capabilities over time. His mindset is focused on progression, and he does not rely on what he has accomplished previously to win. Slater believes, "You should improve forever, and it should be the body failing that holds you back. Hopefully we can all add layers and layers to what we already know. I have more power, better body awareness and equipment. If I'm not surfing better I should quit."

AGE IS A NUMBER

For Slater, his mindset is focused on progression, and it's obvious from his quote that he understands how to build new skills and capabilities. But for Slater, the first comparison made when compared to his competitors is based on his age. Slater has dispelled any myths about his age and performance by proving his worth against the younger competitors within the sport. His main competitor is John John Florence, who at twenty-four is a rising star and just won his first world surfing title in 2016. He is the most dominant surfer of the new generation of surfers, but Slater has been able to match his technical and aerial abilities through skill progression. Slater continues to build upon his years of experience by adding new tricks. His mindset has allowed him to match capabilities with competitors who are half his age and physically more resilient and to tap into the more progressive aspects of the sport.

PROGRESSION AND PERFORMANCE

In terms of performance, Slater has proven he is one of the best competitors on the planet when it comes to surf contests and has consistently come out on top because of his skills and abilities. Early on in his competitive career, Slater was fueled by the split of his parents and used that aggression in the water to win contests. As Slater has aged, his ability to stay physically healthy has been challenged, but his mindset for competition and performance in contests has not. He sees younger surfers not as competitors, but as contemporaries, and he has developed personal relationships with most of them. His approach is more about healthy competition than about dominance, and Slater now uses the age difference to fuel his performances. He says, "I don't care what my age is. These are my peers, and I'm surfing against them. If they have a problem that I'm older, then go ahead and beat me." Slater's abilities and skills continue to progress and evolve over time. The performances are fueled by his mindset to progress his own skills and to stay relevant in the sport he loves.

NEW MINDSET FOR BUSINESS

1. COMPETITIVE ADVANTAGE

MARKET CHANGES

When looking at a progression-based mindset from a business perspective, some of the same considerations that a surfer would make in approaching their sport can be true for the marketing and sales professional. The new business challenge for leadership is that there is constant change to markets in the new conditions. Business professionals will need to adapt to changes by adding new skills and determine which skills will be the most relevant to their specific market conditions at the time. Just as Kelly Slater approaches his skill development as a surfer, business leaders will need to evolve and change what they are doing in order to stay current with what's new by using a new mindset to stay competitive. As the relevant skills and capabilities change, so will an organization's ability to hold a competitive position in the market. Organizations will need to evolve with market changes to fend off new competition.

NEW COMPETITION

In the new conditions, a competitive advantage is estimated to last only six months within a given market. This means that every six months, a different organization will become a market leader, and the advantage that an organization once had will be gone. As technology changes market conditions, advantages will come and go. Competitors will be able to unseat market leaders by unbundling services and offering more specialized services. Organizations that may have owned the entire process related to a transaction will lose their advantage to more nimble players that challenge market leaders for small pieces of the business. New market entrants will be able to capture small pieces of a market, but those pieces will pay off big if they offer innovation and new value that the larger organizations cannot. The competitive advantage that was once held in markets by organizations is switching hands more often, and organizations will need to change their mindsets toward skills to stay competitive.

NEW EXPECTATIONS

With increased competition, the skills needed to meet new customer expectations are changing as well. As organizations try to compete, they also have to meet the new expectations of customers that are buying products and services in a new way. Customers are demanding organizations have new skills to meet those expectations. It's estimated that more than two thirds of sales and marketing transformations fail, with

70 percent of those failures happening due to a lack of the organization's ability to adopt new skills and capabilities.[2] As the competition increases within markets and as customers demand new skills in how products and services are sold, organizations will need to progress to meet those new demands. A mindset toward progression and new skills is critical to the marketing and sales of an organization. Be more like the surfer and change your mindset about how you will compete (and with what skills) and how you will change to meet the new expectations of customers.

2. THE STATUS QUO

RESISTANCE MINDSET

The biggest obstacle for some organizations is not the actual challenge within the market, but the internal struggle to change the collective mindset to meet the new demands. More often than not, this has less to do with the kind of change needed and more to do with the internal obstacles preventing organizations from making a change. This is especially true when the process involves doing something new or different from what the organization has traditionally done. Most organizations stick with the behaviors or habits of past success and do not make strategic changes when they need to. There has been widespread acceptance of new strategies and technologies available to organizations, but there is still resistance to new ways of doing things. Old habits and fixed mindsets prevail in the face of needed change. Organizations often create internal barriers for themselves that are tough to overcome. These new methods have been available for years, and yet adoption is still a mental challenge for leadership that

2 Homayoun Hatami, Kevin McLellan, Candace Lun Plotkin, and Patrick Schulze, "Six Steps to Transform Your Marketing and Sales Capabilities," *McKinsey Quarterly*, March 2015, http://www.mckinsey.com/business-functions/marketing-and-sales/ our-insights/six-steps-to-transform-your-marketing-and-sales-capabilities.

does not have the right mindset or does not understand the business situation.

DON'T UNDERSTAND CONTEXT

Companies are often reluctant to change because they don't understand the new sales and marketing context they are working in. Companies that do not understand the context lack the information and insight to make significant changes. Without market insight and an internal assessment, it can be daunting to evaluate what's needed, and new strategies can seem complex or out of reach. Not understanding the context and having a mindset that is resistant to change can put organizations years behind the market and even further behind competition. Continued resistance causes the divide to become even greater, and that reluctance to change only becomes stronger over time. Organizations then tend to fall back on the old ways of doing things because it's safe and accepted, focusing on well-established behaviors that the organization and the company's culture support. The common response is, "That's not how we do it here." As market conditions change, companies that continue to stay on the same course will struggle in the new conditions. The context within the organization will not support new skills and will push organizations to continue to do the wrong things.

REACTIVE MINDSET

Companies that struggle in the new conditions have a reactive mindset versus a proactive mindset when it comes to new skills and capabilities. A reactive approach to new challenges causes companies to take a "wait and see" or "just-in-time" sales and marketing approach. Instead of trying to add new skills to force the business situation to their favor, leaders do not always proactively look for new ways to do things; they wait for their hand to be forced, only making a change when the new strategy has been proven or widely accepted. These organizations have leadership that's not open to change and has the wrong mindset. When you don't anticipate what is new and make changes accordingly, you lose momentum and any kind of advantage you once had. A reactive mindset may feel safe, but as new challenges are now encountered in the market more often, organizations that take this approach will struggle to find success.

3. THE RESULTS

THE OLD WAY

When a mindset is fixed and not focused on progression, business leaders struggle to adequately react to new market challenges. It becomes easier to adhere to the old way of doing things and to abandon or stray from anything new. Some organizations are not willing to change, and others might be unable to do so because of the barriers created inside the organization that all support the old way of doing things. Organizations become locked into previous methods and don't change their behaviors, with the biggest challenge for leadership being falling back on the old ways of doing things. Companies that are leading within their markets focus on making significant changes in their strategies, but they are able to break away from the past or create new ways of doing things. Organizations that are not open to change and that stick with doing what's known and accepted versus taking the time, effort, and initiative to do something new, struggle and have lackluster results because of this approach.

LACK OF LEADERSHIP

When leadership within an organization knows that the organization needs to change and they do not take the necessary steps to do so, it is simply bad leadership. Leaders are in positions to make strategic changes that will build and grow an organization. Most companies talk about innovation and use it as a tagline for describing how they are different. Most leaders, however, fail to execute on those innovative ideas. If leaders do not have a progressive mindset and do not add new skills and capabilities, they prevent teams from further developing themselves, which stifles the organization's ability to meet new challenges. When leadership does not invest in new skills or capabilities for themselves or the organization, the inability to progress prevents them from solving the external challenges as well. If leadership lacks the understanding of the business situation or the new context the organization is working in, this can hamper the collective mindset of the organization and create bad results in the short and long term.

SELF-PROTECTION

Falling back on the old way of doing things and then not stepping up to leadership challenges is a forms of self-protection. The perception of the risk involved with something new can hinder progression and force leaders to make decisions in their own best interest and not in terms of what is needed for the organization. Leaders often make decisions that benefit them personally in the form of career longevity, pay increases, and holding positions of stature, before making decisions that benefit the organization. But self-protectionism hurts the organization, hurts the business, and does nothing to help the most important group of people in the equation— the customers. Doing things the old way, not displaying leadership during important transformative decisions, and protecting one's own self-interests are the results of not having a progression-based mindset. The organizations and leaders that do decide to adopt a new mindset and learn new skills or organizational capabilities will follow in the path of the surfer and benefit from this new approach.

THE NEW PRINCIPLE

1. HOW TO ADOPT A PROGRESSION-BASED MINDSET

IDENTIFY NEW SKILLS AND CAPABILITIES

With a competitive advantage typically only lasting six months within a market, companies need to be building new skills and capabilities that allow the organization to evolve with changes in the market. Leaders need to adopt a mindset based on progression and adding new individual skills, but also thinking holistically about what kinds of capabilities they want to add within the organization. Surfers have a growth mindset when it comes to their skills. They are constantly trying to evolve what they can do on a board, and they use a process based on skill progression. For organizational leadership, this new mindset will be critical to overcoming the new challenges we are facing and will be needed to support new strategies. For sales and marketing leaders, a progression-based mindset could be a powerful way of thinking about new initiatives and a new way to tackle market challenges.

INVEST IN TRAINING AND DEVELOPMENT

According to recent studies, more than two thirds of organizational transformations within sales and marketing failed, with over 70 percent of those failures being due to leadership's inability to adopt new behaviors completely. This pattern is a result of leadership underestimating the effort required to make significant changes and not having the proper training or support in place to guide teams through the process. In order to compete in the new market conditions, leadership within organizations will need to regularly invest in training and development to support new skills and capabilities. Leadership will need to create a long-term plan around how the new skills will be built into the organization over time. Training and development have become less of a priority in recent years with organizations preferring to poach top talent instead of developing it in-house. However, in order to keep valued employees from leaving the organization, training initiatives will need to be aligned with the current new skills and demands of the market.

CHANGE MANAGEMENT

Identifying new skills is important to the change management process, but so is creating the vision and the plan for how to develop these skills. Developing new skills will require planning and change management strategies to find success. Organizations will need to make the new initiatives a priority, plan for the change, and manage the process, using milestones to track and assess progress. Marketing and sales processes will need to be aligned with the new skills being developed and become part of the culture within the organization. The new skills will need to be supported through corporate messaging and mantras that align with the new way of conducting business. Managing the change will need to be backed by compensation plans, incentives, and rewards. Individual development plans and performance reviews will need to model the new skills and objectives. Organizations will need to incentivize teams not only to change their behavior related to their specific roles within the organization, but also to change their mindset in how they see themselves in their roles.

2. THE BENEFIT

UPGRADE SALES AND MARKETING

Organizations that invest in new skills and capabilities have better results. Of the companies that upgrade sales and marketing capabilities successfully, 90 percent of them deliver above market growth, with 30 percent of those companies having greater revenue than the average company within their sector.[3] Adopting the right mindset and adding new skills or capabilities not only benefits the individual, but also drives bottom-line growth for the organization. Successful organizations start with an internal assessment that reveals the opportunities within teams and areas needing improvement. They also determine which capabilities are having an impact and should be targeted with additional resources. Progression-based organizations view sales and marketing as an investment and not as an expense. They invest in sales and marketing planning tools, software, and training as they identify the new skills that are needed inside the organization.

PRODUCT CONCIERGE

As new sales and marketing skills are needed to align organizations with the new way that customers buy, leadership will have to organize functional areas to support this change. If you think back to my car buying experience, the salesperson I worked with had to adapt to the way I wanted to buy. Since I had done my research in advance through my own self-driven customer journey, this person became more of a product concierge than someone there to sell me something. As markets continue to evolve and change, sales and marketing roles will evolve as well. For organizations, the sales and marketing focus will be on creating an experience for the customer rather than selling your product. Leadership will need to bundle functional areas together and map out the entire customer journey from end to end. The benefit is that organizations will be more aligned with the market and the customer. There's also less transactional pressure, and the organization can focus on educating the customer about the product or service as

3 Bart Delmulle, Brett Grehan, and Vikas Sagar, "Building Marketing and Sales Capabilities to Beat the Market," *McKinsey Quarterly*, March 2015, http://www.mckinsey.com/business-functions/marketing-and-sales/our-insights/building-marketing-and-sales-capabilities-to-beat-the-market.

well as creating a unique buying experience as a concierge.

SKILL-DRIVEN RESULTS

Organizations that have been successful in the new conditions all focus on acquiring new skills and capabilities, but they focus on using them to drive improved results. Successful organizations have leadership that acquires new skills for themselves, but they also adopt needed capabilities for their organizations. They make acquiring those new skills or capabilities an investment and part of the organization's culture. To ensure that they are on track and consistent with the new initiatives, they schedule the change and plan for it. The successful organizations do not try to do too much. They have a narrow focus on what they need and a good understanding of where the organization is in the development process, meaning that they do not try to do things too far outside the organization's capabilities. They develop the needed capabilities in the right sequence and use performance measurements or incentives tied to the new methods to drive results.

3. JOHN'S PROGRESSION

OUTBOUND—THE OLD

After working within organizations for fifteen years, I had experienced the luxuries of having multiple functional teams developing strategies and creating resources to help me do my job. But as I started to explore sales and marketing work on my own, there was only so much time and effort I could dedicate to new strategies and initiatives. As someone responsible for developing and also executing new sales and marketing tactics for my own business, I had to make decisions on how and where I would spend my time. When I launched my marketing and sales firm in 2014, I focused on the activities that would hopefully bring me the most return from my efforts. Outbound activities were the easiest way to start since they were predominately customer facing, but they also provided you with an immediate sense of success or failure. The outbound activities I used included industry events, seminars, networking meetings, distributing business cards or marketing materials, mailing postcards, and making cold-calls on potential clients.

INBOUND—THE NEW

After a full year of focusing on only outbound activities, I was worn out, loathed networking events, and generally had a bad taste in my mouth from the entire experience—not just from the thousands of stamps I was licking for those postcards I put in the mail, but from putting in a ton of effort and not making the dent in the market I was hoping for. I felt like I was pushing a rock uphill, barefoot, and in the rain. The hill was slippery, and I was exerting a lot of effort, but I was experiencing constant slip-ups and little to no forward movement. With nothing else to lose and wanting to expand on my skills and capabilities, I decided to do more inbound marketing activities instead. The inbound tactics I used focused on developing a website and social media presence, using analytics to measure engagement, writing on a company blog, using an email marketing system, creating content and videos, and self-publishing a book. I had little to no experience with any of these things, but I knew that I had to start developing these skills for the future and that they would ultimately help my business.

JOHN'S MINDSET

Thinking about my approach to building these new skills, I realized I had to use what I learned from the surfer. I had to embrace what was happening in the market conditions and change my mindset from having static "outbound" skills to building "inbound" skills that were based on progression. I knew it would be a risk to try and build these skills, but I used the principles of the surfer as the process to help me begin. The process started with acquiring some basic knowledge of what the new inbound tactic would do for my business, a plan for me to start experimenting with it, and then testing it live to see what would work and what would not. Moving from the old way to the new way was hard. But after two years, I had a website, blog, presence on social media platforms, a completed set of videos, and a self-published book. I knew that going forward, my skills could never again be static and that if I continued to leverage a mindset based on progression, I would be able to adapt and evolve with the changing market conditions.

PRINCIPLE III: USE RISK AS A COMPASS

9

SURFERS USE RISK AS A COMPASS

1. SURFERS AND RISK

THE RISKS

Embracing the conditions and building new skills through a progression-based mindset are the first two principles of the surfer, but what separates the pros from the rest of us is their ability to Explore Risk. For surfers, the gateway to success is risk. The more risk surfers take on and explore, the better they become. The more they are challenged to advance their skills and capabilities, the more progressive they become as surfers. Surfing carries a high level of risk, and the consequences from blindly pushing for risk without careful planning can be disastrous. Some of the best surfers in the world have lost their lives when they encountered a risk that they were not prepared for. For business leaders, the most extreme risk is job loss, or in extreme cases, prison for conducting business in an illegal or unethical manner. But for the most part, we tend to encounter more mental hurdles than we do life-or-death situations.

THE IMPORTANCE OF RISK

Surfers are wired differently because of the demands of their sport, and they have been conditioned to look at risk in a different way than most of us. Overcoming risk can be the difference between surviving failure and finding success. When discussing the risks in surfing, it's also important to talk about progression. For surfers, progression in their sport is limited by the amount of risk they are willing to take. If they do not take on and continually explore risk, they will not progress, which slows down their ability to develop new skills. Tow-in surfing and big wave riding has proven that surfers have conquered all aspects of the ocean and surfed waves that were thought impossible to ride, even just a few years ago. By challenging their skills and also their mindsets about what was possible, they were able to take on risk and move the sport forward to create a whole new category of surfing.

SURFERS USE RISK

What makes surfers different from other professional athletes and makes them a good example for business leaders is their approach to risk. Action sport athletes are in one of the few professions that encourage personal risk. The consequences of failure for surfers is so much higher and more extreme than it is for most action sport athletes, but the risks are a significant part of the sport and ingrained within everything the surfer does. The surfer's ability to challenge and confront risk determines success or failure. The mindset of surfers is to evaluate the risk, determine if they have the skills to handle it, and take action in the face of the unknown. As a surfer seeking and exploring risk, you need to accept the risks, persevere, and then push through. This is how surfers use risk to become better and how they benefit from the new opportunities they create for themselves.

2. THE BENEFITS OF RISK

PHYSICAL

Although the risks continue to increase the more a surfer pushes to embrace the conditions and learn new skills, there are also a set of benefits to the sport that develop as the surfer pushes through each new challenge. The first benefit from risk exposure is the physical result of taking on increasingly greater challenges. The more the surfer tackles new challenges, the more physical health benefits will develop as a result. Surfing is considered one of the most challenging sports because of its various physical elements, including cardio endurance, upper-body strength, and core strength. In order to do one of the basic moves in surfing, good total body strength is needed to move from a prone position to a standing position on the board. This makes surfing one of the most physically demanding sports, and for people who participate with the intent of pushing through risk-driven situations, the physical challenges continue to grow the more that a surfer takes risks on their board.

MENTAL

Along with the physical benefits of surfing, there are the mental health benefits of doing something active as well. Exercise and physical activity have been proven to help people reduce stress and become more relaxed as well as to contribute to better overall moods. The same is true for people who pursue physical activity through a sport like surfing. In addition to the mental benefits, there are also the psychological effects of taking on a new risk and the feeling of success that comes from having accomplished what you set out to do. Surfers spend hours attempting maneuvers and trying to perfect new tricks on waves. There is a strong sense of accomplishment that comes from planning a trick, attempting that trick, and pulling it off after multiple attempts and various bumps or bruises collected along the way. Surfers describe that feeling as the "stoke," and experience it when they catch a wave, ride the tube, or land a challenging trick. This stoke provides a sense of gratification and accomplishment that makes taking the risk and the payoff worth the effort.

SKILLS

In addition to the physical and mental benefits from risk, surfers also receive the obvious benefit of building their skills. As surfers increase the amount of risk they take, the benefit becomes improved skills and abilities. Surfers take on risk to do more challenging tricks, such as cutbacks and aerials, but they also take on risk by surfing harder and more challenging waves. Depending on where they are surfing or at what break, surfers will have access to a certain type or size of wave. As beginners, surfers start with smaller waves in low-risk conditions and usually attempt only basic maneuvers. But as they build new skills, surfers search for bigger waves and also try to expand their capabilities beyond the basics. As the sport has progressed, so has the level of risk that surfers need to take in order to become the top professionals in their sport. By big wave surfing in places such as Mavericks and Teahupoo, surfers can make a name for themselves because of the risks and skills involved, and no one is better at this than Laird Hamilton.

3. LAIRD HAMILTON

LAIRD AND RISK

One of the best and most well-known big wave surfers is Laird Hamilton. Laird is considered by his fellow surfers to be one of the most talented and innovative surfers in the history of the sport. Hamilton approaches surfing from a unique perspective and is less concerned with the stylistic aspects of the sport and more interested in progression, innovation, and taking on extreme risk in order to push the boundaries of surfing. Hamilton developed tow-in surfing to ride waves once thought too risky to surf. He created a revolution in the sport that brought big wave riding to the forefront of surfing. According to Laird, tow-in surfing happened organically and was simply a way to progress his skills. However, it also changed the perspective of risk and what was thought possible within the sport. By exploring risk and surfing bigger waves, Laird also improved safety for other surfers by developing a rescue option that was not considered previously—or until he started surfing bigger waves.

LAIRD EXPLORES RISK

Laird shatters the mold of what most people think of in terms of a surfer. He combines his extreme physical and mental strengths with an in-depth understanding of the ocean. He says, "Part of it is the ability to be able to see things differently enough to understand what it means to implement it. When people are innovating something, they usually have that ability to understand it before they see it." Laird understands progression when it comes to big wave surfing and believes there is a safe line you can always take, but that you need to push that line in order to progress the sport. Laird says:

> I always say that people only do dangerous things in three ways; in fear, ignorance or denial. Everyone involved in these kinds of sports has a certain amount of each of those. I think that if you're conscious and you really assess things, and it is a dangerous situation, then you should have a little bit of fear . . . When you see and learn, you skip the unknown. When you don't see, you step into the unknown, and that's usually where a lot of the fear is.

THE MILLENNIUM WAVE

In the year 2000, Laird surfed at a spot called Teahupoo. He caught what would be known as the "Millennium Wave"—a seventy-foot wave that was captured on the cover of Surfer Magazine with the caption "Oh My God" and that would change the sport of surfing from that point forward. It was a perfect union of past knowledge and skills combined with new technology that had not been applied to surfing before. Laird describes his wave at Teahupoo like this, "That wave in Teahupoo was a wave we didn't know existed. And the ability to ride that wave in any form didn't exist either. There was no way that wave could have been ridden without towing in. It was a barrier-breaking moment. It showed me and others that waves like that can be ridden." To surf the Millennium Wave, Laird embraced the conditions, had a progression-based mindset toward his skills, and took a risk to make what was thought to be impossible become something that was now possible.

NEW RISK IN BUSINESS

1. MARKETING AND SALES

NEW CHALLENGES

Most marketing plans fail to produce the intended results. With so many marketing initiatives missing the mark, there is more pressure than ever on business leadership to produce results. This is the new risk within business that we face as marketers and one of the biggest challenges in the new conditions. The knowledge that there is a better chance that a new initiative will fail than it will succeed is not only demoralizing, but it also creates new risk for organizations. With the conditions constantly changing and the need for advanced marketing and sales skills, the risks have become greater than ever before.

We have more technology and analytics available to us, and there is more transparency around our actions that highlight our successes and also our failures. The surfers who expose themselves to risk every time they paddle out into the water have a better chance of catching a wave than we do at creating a successful marketing or sales initiative. It could be argued that the risk profile is actually higher for business leaders than it is for the big wave surfer.

RISK IN BUSINESS

Marketing expenditures hit one trillion dollars at the end of 2016, but most CEOs said that their marketing teams could not explain where incremental growth came from under those plans. Technology has created conditions for business leaders that are now more transparent and also a new level of accountability for marketing and sales. Gone are the days of blindly putting resources against a marketing initiative and hoping the numbers go in the right direction. Social media and software platforms are now able to measure every action a customer takes, and this new pressure to perform has changed the way organizations evaluate their marketing efforts. "Likes," "shares," and page views all inform the marketer to a far greater extent than ever seen before. There is more measurement on actions taken, more transparency regarding activity, and greater accountability for organizational leadership. It has created more risk for marketing and sales teams that will need to take steps to embrace the new conditions, learn new skills to manage the change, and then use this new risk to their advantage.

THE RESULTS

With this new pressure to perform, leaders often succumb to the challenges, focusing on "keeping up" with trends versus stepping out in front of them. They view change of any kind as a risk. They settle back into the old ways of doing things and become content with "playing it safe." With failure rates so high, and now part of the new conditions, managers will avoid trying something new out of fear or to avoid risk in order to spare themselves the personal harm that comes with a failed attempt. With the average "life expectancy" of a marketer at two years, you can't blame them. The risk profile is now so high that it is hurting the way we do business and impacting our ability to create value for customers. Poor leadership, fear of change, and risk avoidance all contribute to the poor results and ultimately hurt customers in the process.

2. THE STATUS QUO

DO NOT LEAD

The organizations that are struggling in the new conditions are not leading, but instead following within their markets. The performance pressure on business leaders to predict and produce results has created an aversion to risk for organizations. Along with a resistance mindset, organizations have created a culture of risk aversion and incentives that reinforce playing it safe. There are no real incentives to lead, and traditional organizational incentives are set up to reward behaviors that do not explore new risks. Marketing and sales leaders will not explore risk that puts the organization in a leadership position because being the market leader is risky. There are challenges to maintaining the lead in a market, and organizations have to be continually breaking new ground to stay ahead. It's a tough position, and companies struggle to embrace the challenges and risks associated with a market-leader position. Instead, they often follow the pack. Maintaining the status quo becomes accepted, and organizations stay away from the risks associated with being a leader in the market.

NOT OPEN TO CHANGE

Aversion to risk is also related to an aversion to change. Change is perceived as risk, and when constant change permeates a market or an organization, the mentality is to "CYA" or "cover your ass." It's human nature, and we avoid anything new that might threaten the established norms. But this modus operandi for conducting business ties the hands of leaders from doing what is right for the business situation. Organizations create systems of "tribes" or like-minded people, and these systems condition people to work a certain way. When you work with like-minded people, it's comfortable and easy because you're not challenged or forced to do things that are new or innovative. You stick with what you know because that's what the group knows. Even if there are problems, the internal systems continue to push the status quo and to push for the same results. This process is familiar and comfortable, even if it doesn't work, and the organization rewards compliance to the old ways of doing things instead of creating rewards for behaviors that are new or innovative.

PRACTICE AVERSION

When organizations do not lead and are not open to new change, they practice risk aversion. To organizations, the risk can be the new change being proposed, the potential impact the change will have on the organization, and whether or not the new risk will fit with the collective mindset of the organization. When the conditions are challenging outside the organization and leaders are not taking the necessary steps to meet those new demands, it can feel as though there's a lack of control inside the organization. This sense of having a lack of control leads to feelings of vulnerability, and risk exposure decreases for the organization while risk aversion increases. The willingness to change and adapt to the new conditions is averted, and risk-free actions maintain the status quo. Having a long-term perspective and making strategic plans for the future of the business are prioritized less because organizations avoid the risks of taking a chance on the unknown.

3. THE RESULTS

POOR RESULTS

When companies avoid risk, they maintain the status quo and often see poor results. Organizations see the kind of growth that only happens as small numbers of new customers are acquired or as a market increases in size. They will not have the big breakthroughs that happen when organizations explore risk and create new products, improve the way they market and sell existing ones, or find new ways to solve problems for customers. In addition to poor results, organizations experience the ups and downs that come with inconsistent performance. When companies are not exploring risk or using it as a compass to drive new initiatives, success becomes happenstance, and results are hit or miss. If there is no consistency with their efforts to explore new challenges, the results will be inconsistent as well. Hoping for better results without doing anything new will not work in the new conditions, and it's a disservice to customers who have much higher expectations for products and services.

TALENT LEAVES

Talented professionals know how important job experience is to their careers long term and will no longer be tied to an organization that does not provide new professional challenges. Top talent looks for organizations that are ahead of the curve, trying new things and bringing innovation to marketing and sales teams. Organizations that stifle creativity and progression with the old way of doing things and have a low risk tolerance for anything new will push talent out the door. Talent will always leave a company for new, better, and more challenging opportunities—especially for more aggressive, risk-driven cultures within progressive organizations. Just as customers now have the power in the company-customer relationship, professionals now have the ability to demand better working conditions, better hours, better pay, and most importantly, better work. If the work does not challenge people's skills, companies will likely have to settle on candidates who do not have the experience for the job, or they will have to hire less desirable talent who do not fit the organization's needs, culture, or long-term vision.

CUSTOMERS GET BORED

If your talent starts to make their way out the door, it's almost a certainty that your customers will leave you too. If you are not exploring risk and challenging the organization on behalf of your customers, they will get bored and leave you for someone else. With the increasing number of products and services available to customers, break-ups between customers and a company are much easier to do. Customers have more buying options, and the trade-off is often a better product at a lower price. If you are not offering value or taking risks on behalf of your customers, they will become disinterested in your offerings and leave you to be with those who are. Customers want to be affiliated with products that are new and different. If you are not willing to change the way you do business and explore risk, the market will weed you out as more forward-thinking and skilled organizations take your place.

THE NEW PRINCIPLE

1. HOW TO USE RISK AS A COMPASS

RISK PLAN

Because of how fast market conditions are changing, leaders need to explore risk in ways that they have not done before. Surfers use risk as a compass to point them in the direction they need to go to improve their surfing and progress in their sport. Business leaders will need to take a similar approach to market challenges in order to identify new opportunities. Risk exploration is the new principle for how we will need to approach the new obstacles we are facing. This new approach will help leaders create new opportunities for the business and break new ground that was once avoided because of the perceived risks. Organizations will need to develop plans devoted specifically to exploring risk. The plans will need to provide a roadmap for exploring new ideas and initiatives and managing the potential risks involved with making these kinds of new strategic decisions. Basic strategic planning is no longer enough, and organizations will need to build risk into plans in order to succeed in these new conditions.

PROTOTYPE

In addition to planning for risk, leaders will need to begin prototyping the new ideas that are built into risk plans in order to understand the new market conditions. This is an "adaptive" or "evolutionary" process to embrace the conditions and learn new skills, but also to use the results of their actions to take progressive steps forward in light of the risks involved. Leadership will also need to build up a risk tolerance for prototyping ideas and be okay with experimentation and the failure that may result during this part of the process. Prototyping ideas in practice will help uncover the risks involved, and as a result, organizations will better understand how new ideas will translate in the real world. This part of the process is important when risk planning and provides most of the innovation and new ideas. Prototyping ideas and concepts will allow you to build confidence in taking on new risk and to develop strategies that better match with the needs in the market.

REWARD

After planning and prototyping for risk, leaders will need to create rewards for their efforts and align incentive systems to support the new risk-taking actions. Leaders will need to clearly and openly create rewards and incentives that support risk and also create the new context in which the risk initiatives will exist. Part of the problem business leaders have had is the repeated failures of new marketing and sales initiatives. Most failures were not the result of poor planning, but of poor execution and not fully committing the organization to the new business context because of the risks involved. Incentive systems, bonus structures, review processes, and even the organization's culture should all support the new context and inherent risks. If incentive systems and processes continue to reinforce and reward the status quo, risk planning and prototyping will offer little support as you explore risk. New incentives built on risk need to keep the organization on track and headed in the new direction.

2. THE BENEFIT

RISK STRATEGY

For marketing and sales leadership, we will need to use risk as a strategic compass that points us in the direction of new challenges, but also new opportunities. Without risk, there will be no reward. Without the trade-off of exploring risk as a strategy to find success, there is no chance of accomplishing anything great. The organizations that plan for risk in order to find success will experience better results compared to those that do not. Of the companies that strategically examine risk, two thirds achieve increased profitability or revenue growth. Of that group, 25 percent of organizations achieve it in both areas.[4] When companies explore risk, there is a good chance that the business will improve. Not only do companies enhance their chance to improve profits, but there is also a good chance that revenue will improve as well. The trade-off is simple, but the exploration of risk is much more challenging. Most organizations are risk-averse and will not openly expose themselves to the challenges associated with risk. In these new conditions, however, leaders will need to take a new approach and explore the benefits that come with risk as a strategy.

VIEWS OF RISK

Organizations that explore risk are more successful. Leaders who have a healthy relationship with risk all approach risk the same way. They manage it, plan for it, and build it into their internal systems. The successful organizations have developed a new relationship with risk and are the leaders within their markets because of this approach. They have given themselves and the organization the freedom to prototype, test, and fail, always trying to move closer to what will best help the customer and also make the organization more successful. Organizations that have a positive view of risk see themselves as "learning organizations" and use business risk to evolve or change. Business leaders will need to explore new ideas, regardless of the perceived risks. Organizations may only have a few chances to ride the wave in a market, so risk is necessary in order to learn, grow, and build something new.

---

4 Homayoun et al., "Six Steps to Transform Your Marketing and Sales Capabilities."

CONTINGENCY PLANNING

Much like a property developer would create a contingency fund for a construction project that could go over budget or accrue unforeseen costs, organizations have to build risk into financial planning and plan for setbacks that may occur because of the unknown risks explored. Leadership will need to work with sales and marketing teams to develop contingencies that will support risk by including "time spent" measurements or financial incentives for trying and failing. When a new initiative explores risk, incentives and rewards should be considered when planning for new risk. If the new initiative struggles because of the risk, the culture, incentives, and rewards all need to continue to support the effort long term. Just like the surfer who continues to progress and learn new skills in the face of risk, business leaders will need to constantly challenge and update plans so that incremental risks are taken and the organization continues to move forward.

3. JOHN'S RISK

A NEW JOURNEY

After working professionally for fifteen years inside organizations, I was ready to do something on my own and begin a new journey. It would be my first experience working for myself, but I felt like I had learned a few things over the years and was at a point in my career where I was ready for a new challenge. Launching a business would be a good change and there would be long-term benefits that come with the experience of starting a business. However, I also knew that I would be taking on new risk—the most that I had taken up to that point in my career. The first thing I did was to begin minimizing the risks as much as possible. The risk plan was based on the initiatives and strategies I would use to start and build the business, but I knew that the financial risks would be the most challenging to overcome. If I could overcome the initial financial risks associated with starting a business, there was a good chance I would be able to have the business up and running.

PROTOTYPE AND TEST

As I started to build the business, my focus was on learning more about the sales and marketing challenges that organizations were facing and developing a solution to help them solve these problems. To reduce my risk further, I began to test and prototype business ideas with personal friends, colleagues, or professional connections. There was a lot of trial and error at this point in the process, with most of my time being spent trying to understand the challenges of the market and what problems organizations really needed solved. I took each encounter, good or bad, as a learning opportunity and a chance to build a business that would be valuable, unique, and relevant to what businesses were experiencing in the market. As I tested my ideas and prototyped possible solutions, I noticed that some of my original assumptions were wrong and that I would need to keep working at the business and testing new ideas until I found solutions that were relevant to potential customers and solved their problems.

RISK AND REWARD

During the planning and prototyping process, I took on risk to test the assumptions that were within my original plan, which allowed me to explore new ideas in the market before they went live. I was able to develop a business concept and began the process of marketing my services. As I started to promote the business, there were challenges and risks associated with everything I did. Now that I was on my own, the risks were greater, the challenges were much harder to overcome, and everything took three times longer to complete than I had planned. Along the way, I tried to recognize milestones and, as much as I could, celebrate the small successes. I had to reward myself for the risks I was taking and create times during the day or week where I would recognize my accomplishments. There was risk in striking out on my own, but there was also the reward of embracing these new challenges, learning new skills, and starting a new business in the face of risk.

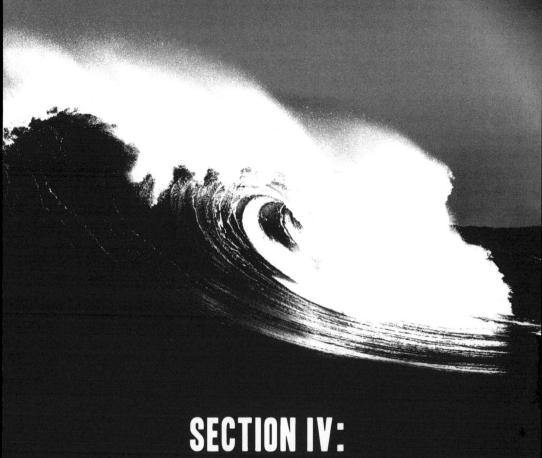

SECTION IV:
RIDE THE WAVE

"Companies that find success during
The Third Wave will be propelled by bold,
ambitious thinkers, people who know how
to navigate a set of complicated challenges
strategically and confidently—and who relish
the chance to do so."

RIDE THE WAVE PROCESS

10

EXTERNAL VIEW: THE CONDITIONS

1. INDUSTRY

QUESTION: What are the trends or new challenges within your industry and market?

The new market conditions have changed the business landscape for organizations. Marketing and sales leadership will need to change their mindset as well as develop new skills and capabilities to keep their organizations competitive. Leadership will need to experiment with new ideas, prototype strategies, and use failure as a way to manage the changing conditions. The three principles of the surfer provide a new process for business leaders to ride the wave of change and find success in the new conditions. The principles can be applied to any new sales or marketing challenge and used as a discovery process to create a roadmap for new strategic initiatives. The first step in the process is to take an external look outside the organization to identify the new trends and challenges happening within your industry and specific market.

ACTION: Industry and Market Analysis

What has happened in the industry or market within the last six to twelve months? What has changed the way customers buy or the way products or services are marketed and sold? What are the trends you need to consider when creating a new sales or marketing initiative? The answers to these questions will come from exploring how market or industry changes are impacting your organization as well as your customers. Exploring the new challenges will provide you with insight into how they are impacting your team members' ability to do their jobs and how customers are finding solutions to their problems. Gaining insight into the trends and changes will impact your strategic decisions during this process. Most organizations are so focused on the internal challenges that looking externally, outside the organization, can be very hard. Understanding how your industry or the market is being impacted by new technology, new regulations, or new trends will be important as you take your first steps with the process.

EXAMPLE:

Organizations can approach the industry and market analysis as a two-step process. 1) Get your teams together to openly discuss the current challenges and the kind of obstacles they are facing outside the organization. The biggest challenge for your teams will be stepping out of the business to think critically about the market or industry and not their specific roles inside the organization. What new initiatives have fallen flat in the last six months? Was this a result of internal failures or were there greater external challenges impeding progress? 2) Conduct informational interviews with customers and ask about their current challenges. Are they seeking alternatives because of new challenges or market changes? Are the internal challenges your teams are experiencing related to the challenges your customers are facing? Avoid trying to sell or market your products to customers, and instead, use this opportunity to understand their needs. This approach will build trust and also give you the insight you need to evaluate the market and industry more effectively.

2. CUSTOMER

QUESTION: How are customers learning about your product or service?

After gaining insight into the industry and market, the next step is to start to understand how customers are learning about your products or services. This part of the process helps you to understand how a potential customer searches for and finds information and learns about your offering. How are they educating themselves during their unique decision journey and what information are they using to make their final purchase decision? Customers are most likely using your website, marketing materials, and sales resources to find the information they need to make a decision. But are there other sources of information available to customers through other channels not managed by your organization? What does the decision journey look like and is the information they are using to make a decision positioning your product or service in the best possible light? Understanding how customers are buying from you will be the next step to better understanding their unique customer journey.

ACTION: Customer Mapping

Customers now have more ways to source information for the products and services they want to buy. Oftentimes, there are channels that provide information that is independent of what you are offering from a sales and marketing standpoint, but that can still influence a customer's buying decision. Customer mapping is another external view outside your organization that specifically looks at how potential customers are working through their decision journey and what sources of information they are using to make a decision. Are potential customers using your platforms to find information and resources? Are they also using competitive or social platforms to find additional information? Mapping out how customers buy will be important to identifying where you are having success but also where some of your weaknesses could be. Customer mapping will highlight the areas you will want to reallocate and add more resources to areas that are working to drive engagement.

EXAMPLE:

A Customer Map can be used to identify steps in a decision journey that may include your website, social media sites, or action taken from an email marketing campaign. Determining the stopping points for customers along this journey will help you map out how customers are buying from you. This process can also be helpful when simply asking new customers, "How did you find out about us?" Customer feedback will help you understand how they worked through a decision-making process and what information they used to make their decision. Keep an open mind because the process may be different than you think. The customers who are no longer buying from you could also give you insight into how they may have changed their buying habits or found alternatives. "I noticed you have not purchased from us recently. Is there something that has changed?" This feedback will give you insight into how customers are buying, but also point you to the areas along the decision journey that need to be improved.

3. COMPETITION

QUESTION: What message is being driven into customers by competition?

Once you have mapped out the customer decision journey and have a good understanding of how your marketing and sales efforts are helping customers, it will be important to know what your competition is doing and how their efforts are impacting customers. To assume that customers are 100 percent loyal to your products or services would be a mistake. Most customers are savvy and use multiple forms of information to make purchase decisions. They usually spend as much time learning about competitors' products as they do about yours. Understanding that customers use a combination of channels to become informed is important. Be honest and pragmatic with the assessment of your organizational efforts, but also understand how competition is influencing the customer's decision. This external evaluation of the market will help you to understand your place within it, but will also help with your understanding of how customers are influenced by the competition.

ACTION: Competitive Analysis

Some of the best information about your competition can be gathered directly from your customers. If they're exclusive to you, ask them why they made the decision to buy from you and what other products or services they considered before yours. Customers will explain the process they took and the information they used. They can also give you insight into how they perceived your competition during the process. As you begin collecting information from your customers, develop a map for your competition as well. Include the information that customers used and identify the points along that journey where your competition was making an impact on the decision journey. Use what you discover to create a map for your competition and identify each point along the journey.

As you start to find places along that journey where you are disadvantaged or not providing any value to the customer, you should improve these areas so that you become more relevant within that part of the customer's journey.

EXAMPLE:

As you are going through the process and finding that your competition is stronger at points along the journey, identify an area where you have an advantage and focus your efforts there. If you are not gaining the insight you need from customers, become a customer yourself. Walk through the process of buying from the competition. Do the research, visit the sites, and go through the process on your own to understand how a customer would buy from your competition. It sounds simple, but we are all consumers, and we do this within our personal lives every time we buy something. The journey is no different for you than it is for someone that would buy from the competition. Make sure you understand how customers buy, not only from your organization, but from the competition as well. What is the journey? How is the competition positioning themselves and their product at each point of the journey? What buying behavior is being driven into customers and is it leading them to buy from you or the competition?

INTERNAL VIEW: MINDSET AND SKILLS

1. MINDSET

QUESTION: What is the mindset of the organization and does it align with the strategy needed within your market?

In the first part of the process, we were able to gain a new perspective of the external industry trends and new challenges in the market. We also started the process of mapping the customer decision journey to find out how your organization or the competition might be influencing certain parts of that journey. The next step will be aligning the organization with the mindset needed to make strategic decisions and to identify the new skills needed for the market. The place to start this internal assessment is with the mindset of the organization. We've discussed the progression-based mindset of surfers and how they are on a constant search for ways to improve at what they do. The mindset of the organization toward new skills is important, and you will need to evaluate your willingness to take on new initiatives in order to overcome new challenges.

ACTION: Strategy Audit

The first way to gain insight into your strategic sales and marketing mindset is to evaluate your current strategies against what you just learned about the market from your external analysis. Are your strategies aligned with the needs of the customer? Are you providing an easy path for customers to find information regarding your products or services? Customer interviews and internal assessments will give you insight into your organization's mindset about whether or not you currently align with the needs in the market, but also your mindset toward building new skills and capabilities to meet those needs. Are the strategic marketing and sales initiatives effective in the market or do you need to add new skills or capabilities? And if you do, what is the mindset for building these new skills? Will this be easy or a new challenge? Evaluating your strategy against the market will tell if you are aligned, but it will also help you to answer the question as to whether or not you need to add new skills.

EXAMPLE:

The first way to discover some insight into your strategic mindset is to ask the people on your teams, "Are you able to do what you think is right for the business? Are we doing everything we can for customers? Or do you feel tied to rigid internal processes when wanting to do something new?" Talking with your teams will tell you if there is internal red tape within the organization that slows down new strategies and makes adding new skills more difficult. Answering these questions will also help you determine if your teams are being held back from doing what is right strategically for the business if the mindset of the organization is not open to new ideas. If your organizational mindset is not aligned with the market, it could be impacting your ability to add new skills and capabilities, but also your ability to be effective. If your sales and marketing teams tell you that they feel burned out and have a lack of satisfaction with what they're doing, then this is probably a sign that your strategies are not aligned with the market, which is impacting the mindset of your teams to change and meet the demands of the market.

2. SKILLS

QUESTION: What new individual skills are needed to align with the market?

A progression-based mindset is needed to help manage the new market conditions and also help you to think about adding new skills. Organizations have teams with specific skills that have made these groups successful. Individuals add value to the companies they work for by continuing to develop those skills or acquiring new ones. As a contributor within an organization, whether you manage teams or work as an individual, you must think about the new skills you will need to build as the market conditions change. Identifying what those new skills are is important, and the work you have done previously to evaluate the market, customer, and competition will point you in the new direction you will need to go. As you start to change your mindset toward progression, you will begin to see your work differently and realize that there are new ways to approach solving your problems. Building new skills will help you do your job better, make you more valuable to your organization, and bring more value to your customers.

ACTION: Skills Assessment

The next step is identifying the strategic skills you want to develop as an individual. Building a new set of skills that are aligned with the needs in the market could radically improve your business and increase the likelihood of finding success. Having a mindset based on progression will help you to identify those skills and to find out what's needed in the market. Based on what you learned from the external analysis, are there skills that you need that would better align you with the needs of the market? If you evaluate or assess your current skills and there's a gap, what is the new skill that is needed to close it? Is there someone inside your organization who already has that skill? Is that person tasked with a different type of work and could he or she add this as another area of responsibility? Assessing the skills needed in the market will be important for your own development, but knowing the current needs of the market could help you to determine if a new skill is needed within the organization as well.

EXAMPLE:

If your individual assessment points you in the direction of a skill you do not currently have, find out if this new skill would be something the organization would want to develop as a special project. Most people want to be challenged and want to feel like they are progressing in their careers. Developing a new skill can be motivating and can also bring new capabilities to your organization. If you do take on the new work in order to build a new skill for your organization, hand off your duties to someone else who is also looking for additional exposure to a new role or skill. If one of those strategies is not an option, find examples of that skill in the market and hire that person to join your team. How often have you seen a marketing campaign and thought, "Wow, I wish our marketing looked like that." Finding out who did that work might lead you to hiring that person or at least finding out more about what individual skills you really want to add to your teams.

3. CAPABILITIES

QUESTION: What new organizational capabilities are needed now and in the future?

As you start to build new skills within individuals and on your teams, you will start to understand what's needed for the organization now and in the long term. You will need to decide which skills you want to become organizational capabilities and start to develop those skills as core competencies for the organization. Just as you have developed new individual skills and progressively built them over time, you will need to assess your team's capabilities and how you are building those skills to support the entire organization. Individual skills will become organizational capabilities, and you will need to consistently reinforce those skills so that they become the core competencies of your organization. Building from skills to capabilities and then to core competencies will support a mindset based on progression and prepare the organization to meet new challenges as the market conditions change. Determining what those capabilities are will take time and careful assessment, but you will want to ensure that individual skills within the organization translate to company-wide capabilities.

ACTION: Process Assessment

After you have assessed the individual skills of your team members, you will need to determine if they are also capabilities of the organization. If a marketer leaves the organization, will you survive or do you need to hire someone to backfill that role or replace those lost skills? An assessment can determine which parts of your marketing and sales process is owned by an individual and which is managed by a larger team. Is there an individual who is the only person who truly knows how that part of the process works? Or is there another person or a group of people who could cover that portion of the process if someone leaves? Just as you mapped out the customer decision journey from the first part of this process, you should also map out the internal process that your organization uses to market and sell products. Where are you strong and where do you need to build out individual skills into an organizational capability? An assessment of your process and how you sell and market to customers should give you the insight to identify the capabilities needed within your organization.

EXAMPLE:

If you take a short-term approach to adding new skills and capabilities or do not think about the impact they will make long term, you will have challenges gaining traction with new initiatives and will constantly be hiring to replace skills or talent that leaves your organization. Do not hire talent just for a role. Hire new talent to fill organizational capabilities. If you hire a person with a specific skill and then he or she leaves, that person will take away that skill too. Think about your hires as filling long-term organizational capabilities. Hire for desired skills, build those skills into capabilities, and then develop them into core competencies. A progression-based mindset will help you to build new skills over time but also help you to turn those skills into core competencies within the organization and be the foundation for exploring greater challenges and increased risk.

STRATEGIC VISION: EXPLORING RISK

1. OBJECTIVES

QUESTION: What will you do differently and how will you explore new risk?

The first part of the process is focused on embracing the external conditions and discovering the new demands within your industry and market. The second part of the process looks within your organization and helps you to identify the skills and capabilities needed to meet those newly discovered demands. You are adopting a mindset toward progression and using this process as a way to build new capabilities over time. In the final part of the process, you will take the new knowledge you've discovered and put it into action. Identifying the objectives, tactics, and projects you will implement, you will also explore new risk in order to be successful. This third part of the process will help you create the vision of what you want to accomplish and will be the starting point for designing the process to explore your objectives regardless of the risk.

ACTION: Process Design

After you have evaluated the external market and determined the skills you want to build within your organization, your next step will be choosing the objectives you want to focus on and creating a strategic process to support your efforts. Your next step will be to create a process that will help you to implement the new objectives and also support the new context in which you will now be working. Mapping out the customer journey and choosing the new skills to add to the organization will have provided you with enough insight into what this new process will focus on. It is now time to develop projects and to decide how your sales and marketing functional areas will implement each of the new objectives. Creating a strategic vision that outlines the new process and the responsibilities within this process will help to support the new objectives during implementation. You will need to identify the key stakeholders responsible for the tasks within the process and make sure that the new objectives are explored, even in the face of adversity and risk.

EXAMPLE:

Designing a process to support the new objectives will be critical to your success, but the new process must also explore the risks associated with your new strategic decisions. Trying to implement your new objectives without updating your process to include the new risks would be a mistake and lead to failure during execution. Working through your new ideas and creating a process that supports exploring the new risk will support you through the next set of steps in the process. To minimize your risks and keep the process balanced, use objectives from each of the areas we have discussed previously. Choose both external and internal objectives that will focus your efforts both outside and inside the organization. For example, choosing an objective with an external focus like customer mapping would be an easy first step in identifying what you need to change internally with your sales and marketing. Your new process needs to support that change, and you will need to ensure that the tactical actions taken by your teams all support the larger organizational objectives.

2. TACTICS

QUESTION: How much tactical risk are you willing to take on and explore?

Within your new process, a new set of tactics will align with your objectives and support your new process. Choosing the right tactics will be important, but taking on new risk will help you to push in different directions than you have previously explored.

Based on what you now know, how are the tactics within your new process going to help you explore new risk? You will want to determine what you will need to do differently now that you have a new set of objectives and now that your process is guiding you in a new direction. A tactical assessment of what will now work in the new conditions will help you to decide how your teams will be executing on your new objectives. Identifying new technology or sales and marketing platforms to help support your teams could also help you accomplish what you have now planned to do tactically.

ACTION: Sales and Marketing Platforms

During your tactical evaluation, look closely at the potential improvements you can make from a sales and marketing technology standpoint. Are there platforms that will support your new objectives, the process, and what you want to accomplish tactically? At each point within your new process, you will want to be critical about how each task will be accomplished and determine if there is a way for technology or automation to support your efforts. Is there a way for a platform to complete a task automatically or a way for customers to do it themselves? Assigning new responsibility or changing how a task was done previously will require you to explore new risk. You will need to let go of how a task was done in the past and trust in the new way that it will be done now, especially when automation or technology is involved and where there is no human touch to move a task forward. Can leads go directly from your email marketing system to your sales teams through CRM? Do they need to be qualified by an inside sales team first or can your account teams manage the task without slowing down the process?

EXAMPLE:

These are questions you will need to answer, but they will make sense after you have gone through the process and when you start to consider whether or not these new tactics will support your objectives. Ask yourself, "Do we move closer to our objectives if we do this? What new marketing or sales tactics are we going to use to support our new objectives?" The old tactics that do not support your new objectives should be removed from the new process. If improved lead generation is a new objective, and the organization wants to improve how the lead generation process is managed, you will need to determine if sales will continue to develop their own leads or if marketing will own this under the new context. At each point of building out your new process, keep your strategic vision clear and design an end-to-end process where the tactics all support the new objectives. The more risk you decide to take with your new objectives and tasks, the more you will increase the likelihood of success and discover something new from the process.

3. PROJECTS

QUESTION: What are the projects that will support your new objectives?

After you have determined the new objectives and the new tactics you will use, you will now want to bring these ideas to life through projects. The next part of the process is to figure out the sales and marketing projects you will need to develop to implement and execute on your new objectives. The projects can be both short and long term, but you will want to think about your projects as an opportunity to do something new and also keep in mind that you will need to explore risk to execute on your new objectives. Each time you begin a new project, ask your teams, "Is there a way we can take on more risk with this project? And if we take on more risk, will it close the gap on our objective?" Like the surfer, you will need to think of risk as the limiting factor in your overall success. The more you are able to push in the direction of risk and do something new or different, the more impact it will make on your customers and the overall success of your organization.

ACTION: Project Planning

The biggest obstacle with projects that involve risk is simply getting them started. Project planning on the front end will help you map out what needs to be done. Prototyping and testing will provide you with the insights you need to feel confident moving forward with a risk-driven project. Once you have planned and prototyped your projects, evaluate the risks against the potential outcomes and what you could learn from them. What would we learn if we go live with this project now? Is there a way to prototype the project and lower the bar or further minimize the risk? Answering these questions during the project-planning phase will help you develop reasonable expectations of your potential outcomes. Remember that this process is a long-term approach and full implementation will take longer than you think. At this point, your focus is on testing and prototyping your ideas and being willing to put yourself in a position to explore new ideas and objectives through a progressive process of risk.

EXAMPLE:

Start the planning process by prototyping aspects of the project, and have all the various moving pieces in place without actually implementing the new initiative fully. Prototype or test small portions of the overall project and see what you can learn from each step of the process. You will want to have pilot teams test your ideas in the real world or in comfortable, low-pressure environments where the risks are low, but where you still have the ability to gain insight from the results. Your pilot teams will test your assumptions and learn some valuable lessons in the process. Repeat the tests and prototype as often as necessary until you make progress toward your new objectives. Change the context within the organization to support the new objectives and create incentives for exploring new risk. Recognize teams for taking on risk that supports your objectives with incremental rewards. Developing tactics and supporting the initiatives through projects will help you to minimize the risk, learn new skills, and progressively build out your business in new and innovative ways.

RIDE THE WAVE PROCESS

CONDITIONS	**SKILLS**	**RISK**
EXTERNAL VIEW:	INTERNAL VIEW:	STRATEGIC VISION:
Industry	Mindset	Objectives
Customer	Skills	Tactics
Competition	Capabilities	Projects

HOW TO THE RIDE THE WAVE

11

EMBRACE THE CONDITIONS

1. CONDITIONS: MAP / MEASURE / PROCESS

MAP: Customer Journey

The Ride the Wave Process focuses on three areas that help you to evaluate the external conditions, assess internal skills, and identify areas where you can explore new risk. The process is a holistic approach to strategic planning and serves as a guide to creating new and innovative marketing and sales initiatives. The process also helps to align your organization as well as your sales and marketing activities with the new way that customers buy. The first step will be to understand the new journey and map out the actions that customers take. It will help you to identify areas where you are having success and areas where you will need to improve how you are meeting customer needs. Once the journey has been thoroughly mapped out and you have aligned your new process with the customer, your next step will be to measure where you are having success.

MEASURE: Areas of Success

As you begin to align with the market and meet the needs of customers, you will find areas where you are having success. As you begin to identify the areas where you are meeting customers' needs, reallocate resources to those areas to help scale those points along the journey where customers are learning the most about your products and services. As market conditions change and evolve, measure your success against your new challenges. As you create new initiatives to meet customers at points along that journey, you can measure the success of new initiatives and compare results to your previous tactics and initiatives. Test new strategies to see if you are able to gain traction, and measure success by using website analytics, "likes," "shares," and comments and see if those results have an impact on sales or revenue results. After you map the new journey, measure the results and use that information to create another new repeatable process.

PROCESS: Repeatable Process

Once you have mapped the customer journey and gained a good understanding of how buying decisions are made about your products or services, you will be able to create a repeatable process to measure your results. For each new initiative, begin by mapping the journey and measuring the results. Use a repeatable process to compare your efforts over time. Make the process an established action within your organization and stay consistent. Remain open to new ways of measuring success, since your process will need to change over time. As the conditions within markets change and as customers find new ways of gathering information to make purchase decisions, continue to make incremental changes to the process and stay aligned with the new trends in the market. Establishing a process will provide you with strategic insights into the market. You can use those insights to make marketing and sales decisions that inform how you identify customers and satisfy their needs.

2. EMBRACE THE CONDITIONS: Marketing

LEAD GENERATION

In order to embrace the conditions, marketing will need to embrace lead generation and assume the responsibility of this important task. Embracing this change will be important since the role has been more closely associated with sales in the past. As marketing technology continues to evolve and focuses on identifying potential customers for organizations, more and more of the lead generation responsibility will fall on marketers. Marketers will need to use technology and marketing platforms to better understand the customer decision journey and where new leads are coming from. Marketing will generate leads by analyzing website visits and using various marketing channels to drive leads to social media and microsites. They will use that data to develop leads and start the process of marketing directly to those potential customers through a nurturing process. In the new conditions, marketers will be responsible for generating leads but also for grabbing the attention of prospective customers and eventually turning them into qualified leads.

QUALIFIED LEADS

In addition to owning more of the lead generation responsibility within the process, marketing will also need to embrace the development of qualified leads. Marketing will use technology to identify potential leads and begin to nurture those leads. Marketing will own the first part of the process and take some of this lead generation work away from sales. Marketing will need to develop qualified leads that have been nurtured over time and then pass them along to sales to be closed. Since marketing will work the front end of the process and develop leads, it will be important for both marketing and sales to have a clear understanding of who does what in the process, why the process is structured this way, and what the potential benefits will be to having marketing develop leads instead of sales. Prequalified leads from marketing will initiate the selling process and help to speed up the conversion process. The leads that are coming from marketing will be prequalified and prepared for the final concierge phase of the process that is closed by sales.

CONCIERGE

Marketing will provide leads to people in sales who will then work the leads and go through the final phase of the process, closing them for business. It will be important that both marketing and sales understand their roles, and there is a clear understanding of what is considered a qualified lead. The new expectation is that sales will serve as a type of concierge for qualified leads. The leads that are from marketing should be seen as potential customers and need to be treated as such by marketing before reaching the final phase of the buying process. After marketing has identified the qualified leads, passing them to sales in an efficient and effective manner will be important. You will need to create a marketing-to-sales process that supports this new approach and embrace the changes that this process will create inside the organization.

3. EMBRACE THE CONDITIONS: Sales

LEAD GENERATION

In order to embrace the conditions, sales will need to embrace lead generation and where that responsibility now lies. Marketing will take over this part of the process and be responsible for identifying leads, qualifying them, nurturing them, and then handing them off to sales. The biggest challenge for sales in the new conditions will be accepting that lead generation will be primarily done through marketing activities and not through sales. Sales will need to work marketing-generated leads instead of self-sourced leads. The major hurdle will be having sales see marketing-generated leads as better-quality leads and that those leads will help reduce the sales cycle and increase sales conversions. Sales professionals have traditionally seen themselves as hunters—hunting for potential leads and then closing those leads. The new conditions will ask sales professionals to be more like farmers and to work leads that were given to them by marketing and through a new lead-generation process. They will need to farm those qualified leads to make a sale instead of trying to find those leads on their own.

QUALIFIED LEADS

The main responsibility for sales will be converting marketing-qualified leads into sales. Marketing will have spent time nurturing leads through a marketing process built around product or service education. Customers will be passed along to sales as leads having a significant amount of knowledge about the product or service and will be at a point where they are ready to buy or make a final purchase decision. Understanding where the customer is in the process and focusing on converting qualified leads will be the new responsibility of sales. Marketing will pass along a qualified lead with a corresponding lead score, or at minimum, sales will know the kind of marketing activities this potential customer has participated in. Sales will know where to pick up with that customer in the buying process. At this point, converting is about understanding what is needed to move that qualified lead to the concierge phase of the buying process.

CONCIERGE

Converting the qualified lead will be the responsibility of sales, and in the new conditions, sales will act as more of a concierge of the final sale rather than an initiator. Converting or closing leads will be the goal, but acting as more of a concierge and guiding the customer through the final phase of the buying process will be the desired result. The salesperson will need to know where the customer is in the buying process and provide the last bit of information the customer needs to pull the trigger and make the final purchase decision. This salesperson will be providing the final piece of motivation, but also helping to create a unique customer experience for the product or service in the eyes of the customer. The role as concierge will help reduce the sales cycle and shorten the time between identifying a lead and closing a deal. It will also focus sales on what they do best—working with customers to finalize the buying process and creating a unique experience.

ADOPT A PROGRESSION-BASED MINDSET

1. MINDSET: SKILLS / INVEST / CHANGE

SKILLS – Identify New Skills

Because of the transfer of power from sellers to buyers, organizations will need to understand the unique journey their customers are taking and adopt a progression-based mindset in order to acquire the skills necessary to meet their new needs. Organizations and leadership will need to continually assess their skills and capabilities in the new conditions. By using a progression-based mindset, they will add skills as the market changes and as new challenges present themselves. Adopting a progression-based mindset will help leadership use what they identified as new skills in the market and start the process of building or developing those skills in-house. Leadership will need to evaluate the external market and then change the way their organization operates in order to manage new change, add new skills, and meet the new market demands. The first step is to evaluate the organization's current skills and capabilities and then to identify the gaps along with a plan to fill them.

INVEST – Training and Development

Leaders will need to be progressive in how they identify new skills and capabilities, but also in how they create training and development programs around building the new skills with the long-term goal of turning those skills into organization capabilities. Organizations will need to create ongoing training initiatives and reinforce the new skills to make them a core competency of the organization. Training around new skills should include marketing and sales teams together and ensure that each functional area understands its role as well as how each group will work together to develop leads, qualify them, and create a unique buying experience for customers. Organizations should invest in quarterly training to reinforce the new skills and also schedule weekly plan of action meetings that will continue to support the new context in which sales and marketing will be working. Training will be needed to ensure that the newly identified skills become ingrained within the new operating context of the organization.

CHANGE – Manage the Context

Assessing the skills and capabilities of your organization and aligning them with the market conditions will require training, an investment in teams, and a commitment to manage the change in a context that supports your new initiatives. Leadership will need to work with teams, managers, and trainers to make sure the new context is reinforced and that the change process is managed properly over time. Creating milestones on a quarterly and yearly basis will help with the management process and keep teams focused on the new skills during team meetings. Communication channels will help to reinforce the new context. Leaders will need to change their approach if dynamics in the market change and continue to fine-tune training as additional changes occur. Stay consistent as gaps between development initiatives can cause a disconnect between what's happening in the market and your organization's ability to handle new challenges.

2. ADOPT A PROGRESSION-BASED MINDSET: MARKETING

INBOUND

In order for marketing to adopt a progression-based mindset toward skill, leaders will need to invest in more inbound marketing skills than the traditional outbound skills of the past. Because of the new way that customers buy and the new skills that are needed to meet their needs, marketing will have to adopt a new marketing process that more closely matches the new customer decision journey. Using an inbound approach to marketing means educating the customer about products and services instead of pushing them through a process to buy. The inbound process is more customer-driven, focused on customer needs, and more authentic in that it puts the customer first, instead of the business goals of the organization. Marketing will take the lead when it comes to inbound initiatives and will manage the first part of the process for sales. The inbound system will be driven by marketing but will need to integrate with sales and their activities in order to make it effective.

INTEGRATE

Marketing will also have to adopt a new mindset in how they will integrate their inbound activities with those of the sales organization. Inbound strategies can help bridge the gap between marketing and sales, improve sales efficiency, and better align internal processes. The challenge with inbound marketing and an integrated strategy is breaking free from the traditional mindset about the tasks each functional area is responsible for in the overall marketing and sales process. With an integrated approach, marketing and sales will work together and collaborate using a single process that aligns activities under a shared system. Training and development will help to integrate processes, and leadership will need to create the right context around the new inbound strategies. Organizations will need to reinforce the approach through collaborative projects and initiatives, at meetings, and with regular communications to ensure that both groups are on the same page when it comes to the new inbound strategy.

ALIGN

The marketing-to-sales process will need to be aligned so that there is a seamless handoff between each functional area as leads are developed and nurtured by marketing and then handed off to sales. Organizations that use more outbound strategies deal with misalignment and have marketing and sales teams working in silos rather than through a shared process. When the process for marketing does not align with sales, it creates two groups working in different directions for similar results within the organization. In order to meet the new market demands, marketing leaders will need to have an open mind toward skills that support an inbound strategy and will need to make sure they align those skills with the efforts of the sales organization. To be effective, marketing will need to use inbound skills that are integrated and aligned with their counterparts in the sales organization.

3. ADOPT A PROGRESSION-BASED MINDSET: SALES

INBOUND

For sales to adopt a progression-based mindset toward skills, they will need to change the type of activities they are responsible for and move away from traditional outbound skills of the past. Sales will need to develop skills that support an inbound strategy that is integrated and aligned with their marketing counterparts. In adopting an inbound approach, sales will need to overcome some of the biggest mental hurdles within the process in order for the new inbound approach to work. Sales has traditionally self-sourced, worked, and closed their own leads with little help from marketing other than the collateral materials that they use with customers. However, inbound strategies push most of those up-front sales activities to marketing. Not only will sales leadership need to retrain professionals that have been selling a traditional way for years, but they will also have to overcome the internal obstacles that a new inbound process can create. A willingness to work collaboratively with marketing will be required to fully integrate sales into an inbound process.

INTEGRATE

An inbound approach will help you to bridge any gaps between marketing and sales as well as improve your efficiency by integrating activities into a single, end-to-end marketing-to-sales process. Your sales teams will need to change how they approach interactions with customers and will need to adopt a new mindset for an integrated process to work. Customers will have more knowledge about the organization and its products by the time they reach the final stages of their decision journey. With an integrated approach, marketing will have done most of the up-front "selling" and will have thoroughly educated the customer about the product or service. Because the process is integrated, sales will know where the customer is in their decision journey and can use that knowledge to create the best experience to finalize the purchase decision. Integrating sales with marketing will make interactions with customers more effective, create a better experience, and align the sales process with the inbound activities of marketing.

ALIGN

Sales will need to align with marketing through inbound activities and continue to integrate their efforts into an end-to-end, marketing-to-sales process. If the sales organization continues to work within the new system using outbound skills, they will duplicate the efforts of marketing and the process will become inefficient. There will be a misalignment between marketing and sales, teams will become frustrated, and they will be unwilling to work collaboratively with each other. Customers will also feel the pain of a misalignment and will be turned off by a product or service where the process to buy is hampered by two functional areas working separately and in opposite directions. Adopting a new mindset about the overall buying process will better align sales with marketing and better meet the needs of customers. Aligning sales with marketing will be one of the first steps to embrace the conditions and help you to adopt a new mindset toward skills that are needed in the new conditions.

USE RISK AS A COMPASS

1. RISK: PLAN / PROTOTYPE / REWARD

RISK PLAN: Plan for Risk

As organizations and leaders continue to move through the process, embrace the conditions, and adopt a progression-based mindset toward skills, they will need to explore risks that move the organization forward. Leaders who want to use an inbound approach and integrate marketing with sales will need to plan, prototype, and test their strategies before applying them to real-world situations. They will need to fail and learn in order to see what will work using a new inbound process and plan for new initiatives by exploring more risk than before. This approach will push the organization to take on new challenges as conditions change and as new skills are needed in the market. Organizations will need to be okay with trying new things and changing quickly to adapt. The first step for organizations that want to identify new opportunities for success and determine where they want to explore risk is to test their strategies with prototypes that pilot and test assumptions.

PROTOTYPE: Pilot and Test Assumptions

As marketing and sales leaders begin to make plans to explore risk, they will need to prototype, pilot, and test their strategies or assumptions. Organizations can begin this process by taking on incremental risk through pilot programs that will help to determine whether to Test It, Kill It, or Scale It. Prototyping strategies will allow your organization to put your ideas into action, see what the results could potentially be, and do all of this in a safe, low-pressure environment. Prototyping a new strategy could take as long as three months using a pilot program, involve multiple functional areas within the organization, and be tested in the market with a select group of customers to see what the potential results might be. A test could be set up as a "sprint" that takes five days and moves from strategic planning on Monday to testing a new idea on Friday. Sprints can be just as effective as longer-term pilots and can give you enough information to help you make a decision. Pilots and tests can minimize a lot of the up-front risk by prototyping strategies in real-world situations.

REWARD: Create Incentives and Rewards

After the risk planning has been completed and prototyping has been done to test your assumptions, organizations will need to reward leadership teams for taking on new risk and create incentives that reward marketing and sales for exploring new strategies. Marketing and sales teams will not explore new risk unless there are incentives to do so and only if the working context inside the organization supports their efforts. Creating the right context around a new initiative and establishing a change management process will be needed to support any kind of new risk you decide to explore. Organizations will need to create shared incentive systems for marketing and sales as they will now be working together and will share in the risk created by new strategies. Prototyping ideas and strategies that are backed by incentives will be the best way to test new ideas and to build new skills or capabilities in the new conditions.

2. 2. USE RISK AS A COMPASS: MARKETING

PROTOTYPE

Marketing will need to use risk as a compass in order to explore new ideas and strategies. Leadership will want to prototype marketing strategies before rolling them out to customers and will have to explore risk as an approach to overcoming new challenges. Prototyping initiatives will allow you to explore risk, but minimize it the more you test your ideas. Marketing can prototype content and messaging to see how customers respond or if they take action because of it. Content can be hit or miss at times and its lifespan is often considered old in minutes or hours instead of days or weeks. Prototyping content with a test market will allow you to test your ideas before they become part of your marketing mix and give you instant feedback before you put the content in front of customers. Prototyping projects like a video series with a small audience will help you to shape the final product and give you the opportunity to work out the kinks before going live with a much larger one.

PILOT

Prototyping strategies and tactics will allow you to explore risk before going live with new initiatives. Piloting is a more formal way to explore new ideas, and this process also allows you to receive real-world feedback at the same time. Piloting a new marketing message on a blog or using downloadable content such as a white paper will allow you to test your ideas with an audience and can give you a form of measureable results. Piloting content on a blog will allow you to track page views, and with downloads you can determine how many customers were willing to provide an email address in exchange for the white paper. Piloting new messages or new ideas in this way will help you make decisions about how strategies will make an impact and give you insight into the kind of response you might have from it. Piloting allows you to explore new risk in a safe environment and to develop new marketing skills at the same time.

TEST

After prototyping and piloting your new ideas and strategies, you can begin to test final versions of new initiatives in order to see which will be most effective. If you have marketing content that you are ready to launch, conducting tests will help you to determine which ones could make the biggest impact. Creating two sets of videos for YouTube and testing them both can help you see which one is the most viewed, liked, and shared or which video might be worth the prime real estate on your website. Running tests on content allows you to see which ideas are worth it and which could be hit or miss. After testing strategies and determining which are effective, you can then allocate additional resources to them. Tests can identify which marketing strategies are resonating with customers and help you to determine where to focus your efforts. Testing is another form of exploring risk, and using prototyping or pilots can help you test new marketing initiatives and lower the bar for risk each time you explore a new strategy.

3. USE RISK AS A COMPASS: SALES

PROTOTYPE

Sales will also need to use risk as a compass to explore new ideas and strategies. Just as marketing will prototype new strategies, sales will need to do the same to reduce the risk of new initiatives. Prototyping new platforms and tools is a good way to understand how your sales teams might use these materials and what aspects of the new tool will be most relevant to their needs. Before investing your entire budget into a new tool or sales platform, prototype its effectiveness with a small portion of your team to find out if the platform gives you the strategic outcome you were looking for. Since every sales force has different needs and its own unique way to approach customer interactions, you will need to prototype multiple platforms to see which one best supports the needs of your sales team. Prototyping will determine which tool or platform will work in a short period of time and allow you to take the risk out of a much bigger decision that could impact the organization long term.

PILOT

Sales leadership should also consider piloting new initiatives with customers before fully implementing any new strategic initiative. Pilots will allow sales teams to test ideas more formally and gain real-world knowledge about which new strategies might work with customers. Sales can pilot webinars about specific customer challenges and see which topics are attracting a new audience. Webinars will tell you who is attending an event and create an opportunity to follow up on a lead that could become a potential customer. Webinars are not static, and you can change or adapt them to your audience as needed. Content can evolve as you pilot more programs, and it can be tailored to specific audiences based on the feedback you receive. Sales can also pilot events with existing customers

201

and use their feedback to create programs that attract a new audience. Piloting events is a good way to reengage with existing customers, but also an easy way to identify new sales strategies by piloting them with established customers.

TEST

As you work through new sales strategies by prototyping and piloting new initiatives, you will gain more insight into opportunities and more confidence in the ideas that you will want to test more formally. After prototyping and piloting programs, you can now test your strategies with potential customers. A workshop will allow you to test materials with a new audience and gain immediate feedback that you can use to improve sales collateral. Testing point of sales materials and collateral is another way to put new concepts in front of customers and will help you to see which pieces will work in other selling situations. For sales, testing a new sales message in a low-pressure environment can help you gain insight into a new strategy, but it is also a way to take on the risk of trying something new. Just like the surfer exploring a new break or surfing a larger wave, you will need to use risk as a compass and test out new sales initiatives with customers in order to find success in the new conditions.

HOW TO RIDE THE WAVE

CONDITIONS	SKILLS	RISK
Map	Skills	Prototype
Measure	Invesment	Risk Plan
Process	Change	Reward

GOING PRO: GOPRO CASE STUDY

12

EXTERNAL VIEW: THE CONDITIONS

1. INDUSTRY / MARKET

A NEW MARKET

The Ride the Wave Process can be used to find new opportunities in any market or industry and with any type of product or service. As an example, let's go through each of the three principles and look at a company like GoPro through the eyes of the surfer. Given GoPro's significance to the sport of surfing, it's fitting to use the principles to examine the company's external and internal challenges. In using the process, we can look at what has caused GoPro's problems and evaluate what the company did to overcome those challenges and find success. From the time of the company's inception in 2002, GoPro has single-handedly created a new category within consumer electronics. GoPro was the early market leader in portable cameras and had cornered the market through incredible hardware and beautiful design. The cameras were durable, could be used in all kinds of environmental conditions, and brought the action sports market to life.

METEORIC RISE

GoPro had essentially created a new market within consumer electronics and was the category leader within a period of a few years. The cameras were used to film the death-defying feats of action sport athletes, who began to self-produce short clips that showed them catching waves, base jumping, and "going pro" in their various sports. The company became one of the most well-known brands in action sports and had the benefit of free marketing anytime someone posted GoPro footage on the web. The company had built its own community, had loyal followers, and created products that gave athletes of any skill level the ability to share their sporting exploits like never before. GoPro focused on its strength—hardware. The company created cameras that were a staple among modern athletes and worn by the most well-known athletes in action sports. GoPro became a household name and the first in its category to capture the experience of action sports and share these experiences with the world.

EPIC FALL

GoPro cameras were originally meant to meet the needs of action sports athletes, but over time, they started to gain mass appeal. Unfortunately, competitors caught on and GoPro had to defend its action sports niche. Competitors with lower cost options started to enter the market, and larger companies with deep pockets were able to offer cameras priced under $100— roughly a third of the cost of a GoPro camera. At its highest point, GoPro stock traded at $87. At the time of this writing in January 2017, the stock was at $8. GoPro had suffered a significant drop in its stock price, and revenue had fallen from $420 million in June of 2015 to $220 million in June 2016. The conditions had changed, and GoPro was too slow to deliver new products and services to the market. The company was left to fight for its own customers and had to rethink how it would fulfill their needs in the future.

2. CUSTOMER

USER OPTIONS

GoPro was the dominant player in portable cameras, but competition entered the market with alternative camera options, and the market became saturated over time. There were numerous user options for customers and offerings anywhere from $99 to $499 per camera. The price point was far below what GoPro was asking for its cameras, and competition was stealing customers from GoPro by undercutting its business with a less expensive option. The market became fragmented. There were too many user options, and GoPro started to lose the foothold it had built over the years. Customers found lower cost options that could match GoPro's picture quality as the camera technology on smartphones improved and became less expensive over time. GoPro had established a strong customer base within the action sports market, but began to lose ground with new users who found competitor cameras cheaper and easier to use. Bigger and more dominant players that started providing new options to users slowly eroded any momentum that GoPro had generated in the mass markets.

EVERYDAY CAMERAS

GoPro wanted to move beyond its niche of action sport athletes and into a more mainstream market to be seen as a camera for everyday use. The vision was to expand usage among consumers doing "everyday activities," but who never thought to capture these activities on camera. With the advent of social media and self-publishing platforms for photos and video, it became more and more acceptable to post self-created content of yourself doing just about anything from running to playing Frisbee with your dog, or even jamming on a guitar in your room. People's private lives became more public, and they needed a way to capture it on camera. Personal cameras became more accepted for everyday use, and cell phones were suddenly capturing incidents never caught before on camera. This would be a new market for GoPro to enter, but providing a simple, easy-to-use option would prove more challenging than anticipated.

SOFTWARE AND APPS

In addition to offering a quality camera at a good price, consumers wanted to be able to edit their footage and turn it into high-quality videos. Unfortunately, GoPro had spent over ten years focused on building cameras, but had done little to nothing to help customers with their biggest need—taking all that high-quality footage and actually doing something with it. As someone who bought one of the first HERO cameras, I too am guilty of collecting hours of snowboard, wakeboard, and surf footage, but doing nothing with it. GoPro needed to bridge the gap between its hardware and the end video product, but had not developed the editing software or applications that customers needed. For a period of time, in order to edit GoPro footage, you needed at least some level of technical expertise. For action sport athletes or to the everyday person filming their lives on a GoPro, editing was an inconvenience and a challenge. It also became a deterrent to buying one as well.

3. COMPETITION

DIRECT

GoPro has always faced competitive threats, but over time, competition increased, and the market GoPro had masterfully carved out soon became crowded. The conditions became more challenging as GoPro began to expand into markets beyond its core customers and struggled to attract customers who were not action sport athletes. GoPro had direct competition from companies that offered a similar product in the same category and that had the same goals of providing a high-quality POV camera for action sport athletes. The market shifted as larger players such as Polaroid entered the market and offered a camera called the Cube, which competed with the GoPro HERO4 Session. The HERO4 Session launched at a $399 price point and was undercut by the Cube, which sold for $99. After multiple price reductions, GoPro settled on $199 for the Session, but the damage was done. GoPro struggled to differentiate itself, and direct competitors saturated the market with low-cost options that eroded its share of the business.

INDIRECT

As GoPro attempted to enter the mainstream mass market, the company faced indirect competition from large, established brands that offered a similar product, but in a different category than GoPro. The action sports market was virtually created by GoPro, and most traditional camera companies such as Sony, Nikon, and Canon had similar products focused on a different customer segment than GoPro. But as the action sport market began to grow, competitors began to market their products as alternatives to what GoPro was offering and had the backing of well-established brands in the camera market. Drones, for example, had been in the market for years, but began to become more prevalent as acceptance of them started to grow. They were never intended to be used to film action sports and had mainly been used for filming aerial views, but eventually, they became an indirect competitor of GoPro. As a result, GoPro had to develop its own drone to enter another congested market, but the company struggled to defend its share of the market as additional competitors encroached on its turf.

REPLACEMENT

Direct competitors with similar products and indirect competition from traditional camera companies challenged

GoPro. There was also replacement competition from products that were in a different category than GoPro, but that provided a camera option that could be used instead. As smartphone technology improved, mobile devices became a convenient replacement option. Consumers with smartphones had a high-quality camera in their pocket. They could use devices similar to how a GoPro would be used, but that took advantage of the capabilities that smartphones offered. The phones allowed for easy capture of activities, the footage was saved directly on the phone, and you could share the footage online or use editing apps to create short movies. GoPro had excelled as a hardware company, but started to lose the market when direct, indirect, and replacement competition started to offer similar products that were more convenient to use and had capabilities that GoPro had not yet conceived of offering.

INTERNAL VIEW: SKILLS

1. MINDSET

ACTION SPORTS

GoPro faced fierce competition and needed to change how it approached the larger mass market. The organization needed to think more progressively about what skills and capabilities would be needed to stay competitive in the new market conditions. GoPro had to change its mindset toward skills and think progressively, like the surfer, about what it needed to do differently. The company was locked into an action sports mindset and had focused on that core audience for so long that it did little to expand beyond its current capabilities. If GoPro was going to progress, it would need to change how it viewed itself and its skills within the new market. GoPro wanted to attract a mainstream audience that would attach a camera to a baby stroller, sailboat mast, or the collar of a dog. GoPro held onto its action sports market, but changed its mindset about how its camera could appeal to the larger mass market.

MIX AND MATCH

GoPro was protective of its cameras and the footage created by its community on these cameras. The company's mindset was that customers should not be allowed to use competitive cameras to capture footage and mix that footage with GoPro footage or use competitive editing and production applications. The fear was that competitive platforms would cannibalize GoPro market share and pull established customers away from the products. GoPro wanted its customers to use GoPro products only, but the company did nothing to offer new products or services to fulfill customer needs. GoPro decided to change its mindset and encouraged users to capture or edit footage on any application that was convenient for them. GoPro also changed its mindset about competitor footage and just wanted footage to be produced, even if through a competitive platform. GoPro's mindset prevented the company from seeing the opportunities created by software and applications. Over time, however, the company began to take steps to address its skill gaps and capability needs.

HARDWARE COMPANY

For years, GoPro had focused on product development and designing premium camera hardware for customers. The company's focus was on premium and high-quality first-person cameras, but little time had been spent thinking about how customers would access that footage or what kind of platform they would use to edit it. GoPro began to see the opportunities of offering premium editing and production applications. Instead of strictly seeing itself as a hardware company, GoPro realized that it could be a content-production company that offered multiple ways for customers to fulfill the needs that GoPro had ignored for so long. GoPro began to hire developers with capabilities that could help them close the gaps on internal needs and changed how the company perceived its own capabilities. Taking a cue from the surfers who they had supported for years, GoPro adopted a progression-based mindset about its own skills and began to build those needed capabilities.

2. SKILLS

LEADERSHIP

As GoPro began to explore new opportunities within the market and changed its mindset about the type of company it wanted to become in the future, the organization started to look internally at its current skills and how to bridge the gap to the new organization of the future. GoPro and its early leadership team possessed a set of skills that helped make GoPro one of the most well-known brands within action sports and also consumer electronics. When faced with new challenges, however, the company realized that it did not have the right talent to execute its desired objectives and that if it wanted to progress as an organization, the company would need to build new skills. GoPro began to add new skills within leadership teams and evolved as an organization. The organization was forced to purge some of the early employees that had helped to build the organization—about 7 percent of its workforce in 2016, but found new leadership that could move them from a hardware company to a modern software company.

HARDWARE

GoPro's core competency was creating durable products with a premium design. This skill developed into a core capability and made GoPro successful over a ten-year period. But as camera technology improved and as competitors developed quality offerings that caught up with GoPro, the company had to lower its prices in order to compete, losing the key differentiator that had brought success. GoPro changed its mindset about its skills and started to think beyond hardware. In embracing the new market conditions, the company realized that it was not fulfilling a major need of the customer and that competitors could solve these needs and gain significant market share in the process. GoPro realized that the hardware-first approach was coming to an end. The company would need to adopt a mindset toward software and develop an entirely new set of skills that it did not possess in-house. GoPro hired developers and added those skills to the organization by self-producing the skills it needed.

SOFTWARE

GoPro needed editing software expertise and began to develop its own talent, but it was taking too long to build those skills. While the in-house approach was the right move, the company soon realized that other companies were already offering editing software and had platforms that would work well with GoPro product offerings. The company thought progressively and realized that strategic acquisitions and essentially "buying new skills" could help fast-track in-house skills and bring editing software to customers faster than trying to build these skills in-house. GoPro purchased two video editing start-ups for $105 million. At the time, this represented 22 percent or almost one fourth of the company's $474 million in cash. Merging the new acquisitions with GoPro's internal software teams allowed the organization to move faster toward building new skills. The company's mindset and willingness to change how it viewed its skills improved the business and built new skills into the organizational capabilities that were now needed in the new market.

3. CAPABILITIES

COLLECTION

GoPro added new software skills by developing talent in-house and acquiring those skills through strategic acquisitions. This process started turning individual skills into organizational capabilities. Adding software and editing skills to the company's core hardware competencies filled a significant skills gap identified within the organization and also solved a major problem for customers. Users of GoPro cameras would now be able to capture, access, edit, and share content more easily, and GoPro would be able to provide an end-to-end process that it had not been capable of before. By changing its mindset and opening itself up to adding new skills, the company narrowed a capability gap between its cameras and smartphones. Users would be able to do everything their phones were capable of, use a more durable product, and not chance wrecking their phones or losing personal data. GoPro also made its new products more user-friendly by adding a display screen to easily select settings and giving the cameras Bluetooth and Wi-Fi capabilities to make collecting and storing content easier.

CREATION

As users collected content, they were now able to use the new GoPro software to edit and produce videos. The software platform gave users a desktop editing experience and provided a content-creation solution that could be used regardless of the type of camera. This gave GoPro a way to monetize a new service that helped to build from its current capabilities as a hardware company to that of a software company. But moving from a hardware company to a software company would not be the end goal for GoPro. Leadership realized that the long-term goal would be to become a content-creation company. This was a departure from its start as a hardware company, but a good move if the organization wanted to stay relevant in the market. GoPro created a platform for its users to edit their footage, but also created a way to have non-GoPro users try its software and even buy one of their cameras. Adding software as a capability closed a significant skill gap, but it also created a gateway product for new customers to find out about GoPro.

SHARING

After solving the content collection and creation challenges, GoPro next looked at easy ways for customers to post and share their videos. GoPro realized that the market had progressed to the point where virtually every cell phone on the market had both Bluetooth and Wi-Fi capabilities. GoPro began adding those capabilities to cameras so users could upload and share videos without having to use a desktop computer. GoPro also created a platform designed to be an all-in-one platform for videos to be uploaded, edited, and shared. The new offering is called GoPro Plus and is a subscription-based model that allows users to do editing and production within a single platform. No longer are users mixing and matching platforms and applications; they are using a single site and leveraging cloud storage so they have all their video content in a single place. Even with this success, GoPro would still need to explore risk and take on new challenges without letting the market waves wipe out the company.

STRATEGIC VISION: RISK

1. OBJECTIVES

PORTFOLIO

After examining the market conditions and identifying areas where the company could add new skills and capabilities,

GoPro began to take action and implement its main strategic objectives. In addition to adding new skills and capabilities, GoPro needed to create a broader product portfolio. For years, GoPro did not expand its product offerings. However, the company had reached a point where it would need to recalibrate the business and move from a hardware company to a software company. GoPro focused on product development in-house and acquired new products to build a more diverse portfolio. The focus was on new products, new platforms, and new partnerships that would grow the company. For GoPro and its leadership, these new priorities and objectives involved a tremendous amount of risk. But like the surfer, GoPro used risk as a compass and explored adding new products to its portfolio. Stepping into untested waters was a new risk for the company, but one that it needed to take.

MASS MARKET

GoPro firmed up the back end of the content-creation process by offering software and additional applications to provide a full end-to-end solution that competition did not have. The company was creating a new set of products, which was risky, but so was wading into the deep waters of the everyday camera market. Mass retailers favored the larger companies that had deep pockets and established brands. GoPro was attempting to expand beyond action sports and wanted to become a solution for consumers in the mass market. This was a major risk. The everyday camera market was highly fragmented, cost sensitive, and had aspects of seasonality that could create all-or-nothing scenarios. GoPro would need to capture a significant portion of its sales during the second half of the year and during the holiday selling season. GoPro already had its HERO4 Session launch undercut by Polaroid, and mass-retail competitors could do the same to prevent the company from gaining additional ground in the market.

INTERNATIONAL MARKET

As the domestic market became tighter and more fragmented, GoPro began to consider markets outside the United States. The international markets were at least one to two years behind the markets in the United States, which gave GoPro the time to develop a retail plan for capturing international business. The two markets outside the United States that offered the most opportunity for growth were Europe and China. GoPro began to build out a retail footprint for Europe and China as well as developing the marketing channels that would be needed to drive the business. These new markets were developed and mature, but GoPro represented a fresh entrance into the established electronics market. This was another major risk for GoPro, but entering the new market conditions, with a new set of skills and capabilities, would help make GoPro more effective with its tactics.

2. TACTICS

PRODUCTS

In taking on new risk, GoPro aligned itself with what was changing in the market and started to add new products to its portfolio. Product expansion was a strategic objective for GoPro, but tactically, this approach worked to create a new way to offer new platforms and services. GoPro made its new products mobile-friendly and had a solution from capture all the way to the end production process. New cameras also have touchscreen capabilities, voice control, and a wireless remote that provides mobile, but also offers hands-free use. GoPro also developed the Quik Key that allows footage to be transferred from a HERO camera to a phone via an external flash drive. There is also a live broadcast feature on all new cameras and a Quik App for mobile editing. GoPro is offering mobile products and on-the-go content creation that eliminates other platforms from the equation. The company has introduced new products that serve the market better and encourage end-to-end storytelling on a single GoPro platform.

PROMOTION

GoPro had developed the products to support users, but also the marketing capabilities to drive product promotion. GoPro has a unique relationship with its users in that the videos created by surfers and base-jumpers all create free marketing content for the organization. Digital marketing is driven by users who post videos to their YouTube or Vimeo pages and show potential GoPro customers how they can also "GoPro" by capturing their exploits on the devices. By providing new product options that make it easier to create and produce content, GoPro was essentially supercharging its already powerful marketing and sales engine with customer-produced content. The company was also able to leverage the new market conditions created by social sharing platforms to promote these videos to a wider audience. By adding new products to the portfolio, which allowed for easy sharing, and using one of its core capabilities of marketing promotion, GoPro was minimizing its risks through new product tactics and promotion.

PEOPLE

In order to execute these various strategic objectives and tactical initiatives, GoPro needed to hire, train, and develop the talent to execute on the vision. From a tactical perspective, GoPro has had the ability to pull core users into the organization from the action sports arena and retained its authenticity to a community of people who are dedicated to capturing their lives on cameras. From a people standpoint, the company has a tactical marketing advantage because the core users of the products are also the best talent for the organization. GoPro has a relationship with the end user of its products that is stronger than any other company in business today. GoPro has built out its product offerings and focused heavily on new technological capabilities, but the next area of focus will need to be on its people. GoPro needs to go back to what made the company so successful, providing tactical, on-the-ground marketing and sales to consumers directly from its own people.

3. PROJECTS

NEW PRODUCTS

GoPro identified areas where it needed to match the needs of the market and created a set of tactics to help execute on these new objectives. This process involved acquiring new skills, but also building new core competencies that would align them with the needs in the market. GoPro continued to explore risk, change its mindset, and look out at the horizon to find the next wave. One of those next waves was a virtual reality project and a device that had multiple cameras bundled together to capture a 360-degree view. The Omni and Odyssey started out as projects but became reality as GoPro continued to evolve as an organization. After hardware and software, making the move into VR was an easy decision for GoPro. Exploring risk with a new product was also necessary for GoPro to stay competitive. GoPro learned from its past mistakes about not reacting to the changing conditions sooner. The company is firmly in the middle of what's next in VR and positioning itself to tackle each new market challenge as it arises.

NEW PROMOTION

GoPro continued to evolve its marketing and sales as well as the way the company engaged with its user community. Promotion focused on attracting new customers that had not used a GoPro camera before, but also on having existing customers upgrade to newer hardware and take advantage of improved product offerings. GoPro started offering free two-day shipping and free returns on all orders, which made it easy to order cameras and less of a hassle if you needed to make an exchange. GoPro also created new promotional opportunities to motivate consumers to pull the trigger on new cameras and continued to target the mass-market audience, using opportunities to showcase the products in new ways. The movie *The Martian* has extensive GoPro filming throughout and highlights the daily uses of the camera by an astronaut. Matt Damon is a ways away from the action sports market, but the movie was a creative way to promote the cameras and also an easy way to demonstrate these capabilities.

NEW PEOPLE

GoPro created a new set of products for customers, but had entered into a new arena where technology and software could create more challenges for users. GoPro developed options for users who needed to have problems resolved and questions answered. GoPro created support tools in the form of FAQs, customer service lines, and online chats to help customers resolve issues with their hardware or software. GoPro also conducted brand ambassador sessions for its professional action sport athletes to try new products and even brought CEO Nick Woodman to these sessions to help work through the capture and creation process. GoPro embraced the new and changing conditions by finding out what the customer needs were and determining that the company needed a new set of skills to execute on its objectives. GoPro changed its mindset about the organization and began to take on more and more risk in order to close in on its vision. Using risk as a compass, the company was able to bridge market and skill gaps that had previously challenged the organization and set a new course for the future.

SECTION V:
UNIVERSAL STOKE

"When you come to a crossroads, you can either be crippled by doubt, or you can start down an inspirational new path. You have to put one foot in front of the other and remind yourself that there are no wrong choices."

—Maynard James Keenan

SURF STORY: PART II

13

EMBRACING THE CONDITIONS

1. MAP: WATCH AND LEARN

SLAMMED ON THE BEACH

After spending four weeks putting together a plan to surf in the ocean, I made my first attempt in Malibu and found out that the conditions were much more challenging than I had anticipated, my surf skills were severely lacking, and I had not thought about the risks until I was almost drowning in the Pacific Ocean. Once I was safe and back on the beach, I sat there for a while, thinking about what had just happened and where I went wrong in my planning process. On paper, my plan was solid. But in reality, the conditions were much more challenging than I had expected. I wanted to salvage my first surf attempt, learn something from the experience, and then build some momentum for the next time I paddled out into the water. I watched the other surfers who were having success and noticed a specific set of steps that the surfers would take to catch a wave. As I watched and learned, I broke down the process and mapped out what the good surfers were doing.

THE SURFER'S JOURNEY

The good surfers would all take a similar journey to catch a wave. It started with preparation on the beach. Surfers would stop on the beach just before entering the water, prep their gear and board, and also spend a few minutes navigating the conditions and developing their path to enter the water. In Malibu, I noticed surfers would enter the water at either the south end or the north end of the beach. They would paddle around the outside of the incoming waves and into the line-up. The indirect route to the line-up took much less effort and was much safer, and surfers had no need to duck under the incoming waves. Once in the line-up, surfers would sit or lay on their boards in a relaxed and comfortable position, scanning the horizon for breaking waves. Surfers were exerting very little effort and using this time to catch their breath from paddling and stay calm as they waited for waves.

EMBRACING THE CONDITIONS

Surfers were constantly navigating the waves and embracing the changing ocean conditions. Waves or no waves, surfers stayed in the water and were as close to the line-up as possible. When things got hairy and large sets of waves came through, the surfers dealt with the risks or the new challenge and then went right back to maintaining their position in the line-up. There were times when large sets rolled through and cleared the line-up, but within a few minutes, the surfers were back into position and ready for the next wave. As waves came in, surfers would either try to catch them or steer clear of the waves they couldn't handle. They would repeat this process over and over throughout their time in the water and embrace whatever change in the conditions came their way. The good surfers made it look easy and showed the experience they had accumulated over the years of being in the water, embracing the conditions and learning where to look for opportunities to catch waves.

2. MEASURE: FIND OPPORTUNITIES

SMALL STEPS

As I watched the surfers and mapped their journey, I started to gain confidence in my knowledge about the conditions and decided that I had enough information to try surfing again. I grabbed my board, walked down to the far end of the beach, and paddled around the outside of the impact zone toward the line-up. Working my way out to the line-up, I took small and calculated steps. I just tried to do one thing at a time and focused on staying calm, safe, and measured with my actions. As I paddled, I tried to be as efficient as possible and only exerted as much effort as was needed to keep me moving. I stopped to take breaks on my way to the line-up and either sat on my board or lay down flat on my stomach. Just like the surfers I had watched from shore, I scanned the horizon for waves and also took non-verbal cues from my fellow surfers who were watching for the incoming waves as well. I was able to make my way into the line-up and stayed just on the edge of where the other surfers were and also where waves were breaking.

THE LINE-UP

Watching the line-up from the beach, I remembered seeing an informal process for catching waves. It was a first-come, first-serve process, and "snaking" someone else's wave who had been waiting in the line-up was a bad idea. Paddling into waves when it wasn't your turn was an easy way to upset the other surfers. In the line-up, I was patient, respected the space of other surfers, and waited for waves that were at my skill level—not too big and not too small, but enough of a challenge where I could make an attempt at paddling in and try to catch a wave. During this part of the process, I sometimes stayed away from waves. If they were too big, or if a surfer had caught the wave further up in the line-up, I would paddle out of the way, trying to be as respectful as possible and also keep myself safe. Once other surfers in the line-up noticed my etiquette toward the group, there were some surfers who were helpful and threw out suggestions, warning me if a wave was "inside" and helping me to a safe area if I got trapped in the impact zone.

MEASURING UP

As I started to make progress with the small steps, I noticed that I was better understanding how the waves were breaking. I was better at managing the conditions. My paddling and pop-up onto my board started to improve. I could see how I was measuring up to the other surfers. I was actually participating in the process of catching waves, which was a huge improvement from my first attempt, where I spent most of my time trying to keep my head above water. It was helpful to watch others and to learn from what they were doing, but there were also things I just picked up or figured out intuitively on my own. As I tested myself and failed, I started to learn what would work and what would not. I focused on the areas where I was having success and repeated the process until I was catching waves. I was using the other surfers in the conditions as a guide or a way to measure where I was and where I was having success.

3. PROCESS: REPEATABLE PROCESS

TEST, FAIL, LEARN

The more time I spent in the water, the more I understood what was happening around me. I went through the same process each time I was ready to catch a wave and took the same steps to work my way back to the line-up and in position for the next wave. I was testing myself, learning a few new things each time, and figuring out the best approach to use. I tested myself with bigger waves and explored different positions in the line-up. The more new knowledge I accumulated, the easier it became to recognize patterns that were happening in the water. I was building new skills and leveraging what I learned each time I tried to surf another wave. Prior to this second attempt, I was thinking irrationally about things such as sharks, jellyfish, and monster waves sending me to the bottom of the ocean floor. After being in the water and becoming more comfortable with the conditions, I thought less and less about the dangers associated with what I was doing and more and more about my performance and what I was trying to accomplish.

NEW KNOWLEDGE

My knowledge related to the conditions started to build, and I was reacting to the conditions without thinking about what I was doing. I would reach certain parts of the shallows and realize that I had been through this spot before, I could stand here, or a certain area had more rocks than others. Or I recognized that a good surfer had a chance of catching an approaching wave and that I should probably stay out of the way. By spending more and more time in the water, I started to build new knowledge or what surfers refer to as wave knowledge. The wave knowledge I was acquiring grew my confidence, and I could see that my skills were starting to progress as well. Even though I had spent so much time participating in boardsports over the years and was pretty good compared to most people, I was still building new surfing skills, and as the conditions became more challenging, the skills I needed to learn were more demanding.

NEW SKILLS

As I repeated the process of paddling into the line-up and catching waves, I learned something new each time and continued to expand on these new skills I was building. My swimming and paddling needed the most improvement. To help with this skill, I watched other surfers and noticed they would lift their feet out of the water and not let them drag behind. This took some effort and a good amount of core strength since you could not use your legs to balance in the water behind you. It created less drag and faster paddling speeds, but was much harder. I had a fellow surfer give me some pointers on my paddling. He made a gesture to me and pointed to his arms for me to watch. With fully outstretched arms, he was thrusting into the water and pulling himself along the water instead of slapping at it. After trying to catch a few more waves using what I had learned and feeling much better about my second attempt, I decided that this would be enough for today and that I had some new knowledge and skills to build on.

ADOPTING A PROGRESSION-BASED MINDSET

1. SKILLS: CHANGED MY MINDSET

NEW APPROACH

The new approach that I took was to use a repeatable process where I was embracing what was happening and trying to progress my skills each time I caught a wave. Getting back into the water and risking my life to surf again helped me change my mindset about how I could improve. After my first attempt, I learned what skills I had, where my skill gaps were, and which skills I needed to improve. I didn't know I was deficient in these areas until I tested myself in the conditions. I embraced the conditions and did my best, even in the face of what, for me, was an extreme risk at the time. During my second attempt, it was easy to see that I was no Laird Hamilton, and I would most likely not pursue a professional career in surfing, but this challenging experience helped me to learn what I needed to improve. I took the new knowledge that I had gained and used it as a way to build up my identified new skills for my next attempt.

SKILLS ASSESSMENT

Before I started to build my new surf skills, I really had to change my mindset about what I thought I was good at and the kind of skills I needed to develop. Going into the first attempt, I was overly confident in my boardsport abilities and thought my past experience would be a strength in surfing. However, I soon realized that what I thought I was good at was only partly transferrable to the sport of surfing and that the conditions were far more challenging than I had anticipated. After floundering around in the ocean and then slowly working to build some new skills with my second attempt, I needed to assess what next set of skills I would acquire if I was going to try surfing again. I identified the new skills to build and realized they were not a natural part of the boardsports I had done over the years—specifically, my arm strength for swimming and paddling, my breathing, and having the total body strength to pop up quickly and stand on a board.

COMMITMENT TO CHANGE

I knew I would have to change my mindset about these skills and commit to building them if I was going to be successful. The new skills were swimming and paddling, and I had spent little to no time ever developing these areas for surfing. Without access to an ocean or a pool, I realized I would need to be creative if I wanted to find opportunities to build these skills. I was committed to working on these aspects of my skill development and knew that if I could improve my swimming, my next attempt would be a much better experience. I developed ways to build my arm strength without a pool and also worked on my breathing to help my swimming. I would need to be able to stay underwater, holding my breath, for extended periods of time. After this assessment, I also needed to do more training that would build more total body strength. Again, without access to true surf conditions, I knew it would be challenging to do, but I was committed to figuring out how I could start to build these new skills.

2. INVEST: WORKED ON SKILLS GAPS

ARM STRENGTH

After my assessment, I realized immediately that my swimming skills and paddling were pretty poor. Well, actually, non-existent. Not having spent much time in the ocean, I learned to swim in pools, and most of the recreational swimming I did was in a lake at the family cabin. Even then, I was swimming only a few feet and not doing it for survival. Needless to say, swimming in a lake or pool is much different than the ocean. You have controlled conditions for both, and with pools you have lifeguards watching over the swimmers. In the ocean, for the most part, you are on your own. To build my arm strength, specifically my swimming and paddling capabilities, I tried to practice the motions first and then worked on trying to recreate the conditions. I practiced the skills on dry land first and would then try in either a lake or pool. I used a wakesurf board or a stand-up paddleboard in the water, and I would simulate the surf techniques of paddling and try popping up.

LUNG STRENGTH

In addition to my arm strength, I knew I would have to improve my breathing as well, which included my swim cardio and my ability to hold my breath underwater. During my first attempt at Malibu, I got caught in the impact zone and took multiple waves on top of my head. After being held under by multiple waves and not being able to take a full breath, I really struggled to stay calm and relax in the water. Not only did I struggle cardio-wise when I was paddling and swimming, but I was not able to hold my breath for extended periods of time. In building my new skills, I started to work on my breathing and being more comfortable in the water. I was mindful of my breathing while working on my swimming and paddling, but I also worked on my breathing while building my arm strength on dry land, trying to coordinate my breathing with my arm strokes and being conservative with my air. Building my lung strength took time and effort, but I knew this was an investment I had to make if was going to improve my surfing.

TOTAL BODY STRENGTH

As my breathing got better, and I was able to hold it for longer periods of time, I started to work on my ability to pop up or stand up on a board. Completing a pop-up on a surfboard takes balance, but it also takes total body strength since the motion or action is a single maneuver using your upper body, core, and lower body to move from a prone position to a standing position. What makes this move even more challenging is having to do it on a moving wave that is pushing you a few miles per hour over rocks and reefs and past other surfers. It's a physical maneuver, but it takes a lot of mental focus. I practiced the pop-up on flat ground first and then moved to a BOSU ball before trying an old surfboard in the water to get the action down. The paddling and breathing were challenging enough, but the pop-up proved to be much harder than I thought and even tougher when trying to do it on the water.

3. CHANGE: MANAGED THE PROCESS

TRAINING

Having identified three main areas that I wanted to focus on and starting to work on each of them in practice, I realized I would need to put together a more formal plan for my training. I developed a program that I could use to focus specifically on building my upper body strength, breathing, and ability to do a pop-up onto my board. Since these were skills that I would be building for the first time, I knew they would be a challenge and were not natural things for me to do. They were slightly alien to me because of my lack of real surf experience, and it would take some effort to learn. I would also not have the context needed to reinforce them—real surf conditions. But I knew that having my mindset in the right place and trying to create the right context with what I had available would be helpful. After putting my training program together, I came up with some easy ways that I could test what I was working on and use other boardsports to recreate the surf training.

BOARDSPORTS

Even though I couldn't train in the ocean every day, I could simulate the actions of paddling, swimming, and breathing by doing some complementary fitness activities. I would also need to do other boardsports if I was going to make the most of my training. I mapped out a full year with a training calendar and broke down each of the seasons by boardsport discipline. In the fall, I could skateboard. In the winter, I could snowboard. During the spring and summer, I could wakesurf, wakeboard, and wakeskate. I had enough boardsport options to recreate a surf context and use the sports to bridge the gap between my training and my next attempt at surfing. I focused on getting my mindset to a place where I was learning new skills and capabilities, including better balance and agility on a board.

DAILY PRACTICE

Having identified the boardsports that I had access to and adding them to my training plan, I now had a full-year plan to build new skills. I worked on these skills by creating opportunities for daily practice. I would have to make an intentional effort toward the new skills every day, even if just for a few minutes or an hour. This approach would help me to progress my training and also make a big improvement in my surfing the next time I went out. My weekly calendar was organized so that on Monday, Wednesday, and Friday I worked on my upper body, lower body, and total body workouts. On Tuesday, Thursday, and Saturday I did whatever boardsport was in season at the time. The goal was to focus on the areas I had identified as opportunities for improvement, using the training program to keep me focused and to manage the change process.

USING RISK AS A COMPASS

1. RISK PLAN: PLANNED FOR RISK

LOWER THE BAR

By training and participating in boardsports on a regular basis, I was able to build my new skills. I kept trying to improve my skills and abilities each time I trained, but I focused on progression and doing more reps from session to session. If I did 50 arm paddles on the ground, I would then try to do 50 on a BOSU ball. If I did 75, then I would try for 100. This was a great way to lower the bar for risk since I was progressively increasing how challenging I made the training. I also found that the more strength training I did, the more risk I could explore with the boardsports. These two areas fed into each other. When I was training in the gym, I was able to work on skills that I could use in my next wakeboarding session. I could plan for what I would do the next time I was out on my board, using what I did in the last training session to lower the bar and take on more risk when I was on my board.

PLANNED FOR RISK

Instead of doing the same wakeboard routine or the same set of tricks, I would plan in advance what my next set of tricks would be. I planned for the possible risks with each new trick and worked within the new parameters I set in order to build the next new skill. The biggest challenge was not the physical aspects of the training, but when my training would plateau or I would hit a stretch where I was not moving forward. It was frustrating, and my progression seemed to stall. In those situations, I would plan for how I could progress, even if by just a few small steps. It was hard to bridge the gap from where I was to where I wanted to go. In order to get there, I really had to think about the smallest next step I could take. Some new skills seemed out of reach at first, but as I mapped out how I would build each new skill, I started to close the gap and move closer each time I tried something new.

RISK VS. PROGRESSION

The risk began to increase when I stretched myself or when my training did not support what I was trying to do on the board. I had to balance the risk with the progression and figure out for myself, "How can I try this and not hurt myself? What's an easy way for me to move forward while minimizing the risk I'm exposing myself to, but still trying something new?" This took planning, some forethought, and a few extra steps at times to move forward. But as long as I was progressing and learning from what I was doing, the whole process informed future training and the skills I was building at the time. The training program helped me to manage the process, but there were also times when I had to set it aside if something I was trying was not working. Again, my mindset was focused on progression and moving forward, and if that was not happening, then I had to become creative and test new ideas before putting them into practice.

2. PROTOTYPE: TRIED NEW THINGS

PROTOTYPE

The more I trained and made progress, the stronger and more confident I became with what I was doing. At some point, I would need to put my training and planning into action, so I looked for ways that I could prototype the paddling, the pop-up on water, and everything that I had been working on while training. I wanted to test myself in action, but in a safe environment where the risk was low. So I prototyped my paddling by renting a stand-up paddleboard at Lake Calhoun in Minneapolis. The rental shop was a short walk from my place, it was inexpensive to rent a board, and I could work on my balance on a larger board as well as drop down to my stomach and simulate paddling on the water. The lake was calm, and I had the shoreline to shelter me from the wind and large sailboats. It was an easy, low-risk way I could prototype the training—specifically the paddling.

PILOT

After prototyping my paddling on the water, I needed to pilot my pop-up. The pop-up was a tricky maneuver on dry land and even harder on the water. It's a combination of using upper body strength, balance, and good timing to pop yourself up at the right moment, landing squarely on your board and in the right position. I needed to pilot this move in a risk-free environment, but also needed to progress beyond a static gym floor. I did this behind my boat when I was wakesurfing, on a bigger lake this time—Lake Minnetonka. The next time I went out, instead of starting from a sitting position, as I would for wakeboarding, I lay down on the board as I would for ocean surfing. When I got pulled into the wave, I threw the rope and popped myself up like I would on a surfboard. After a few attempts, I started to learn the maneuver and was successful in getting myself up and into the wave.

TEST

After prototyping my paddling and using a wakeboard boat to pilot my pop-up, I needed a way to test what I had learned, but in real surf conditions. I wanted to test my new skills but avoid exposing myself to a large amount of risk. I decided to take a trip to Orlando, Florida, and visit Disney's Typhoon Lagoon water theme park. This man-made wave would be as close as I could get to real surfing without having to get back into the ocean. I would not need to worry about the dangers of the ocean and could focus on my surfing by putting what I had learned into action. I could repeatedly test my paddling, breathing, and pop-up in real surf-like conditions. At Typhoon Lagoon, I tested what I had been working on and got a feel for what it was like to paddle into a breaking wave, gain momentum from the wave itself, and then pop up to ride down the face of it. Testing what I learned was helpful and gave me new knowledge that would help me to close the gap on my new skills before I made my second attempt in the ocean at Malibu.

3. REWARD: TOOK ON RISK

THE RETURN

After spending a full year working on my new surf skills and prototyping as well as testing those skills in practice, I needed to reward myself for the progress I made and go back to Malibu for another attempt. After my first experience a year prior, I knew the logistics and basics of traveling to the beach and how to put myself in a position to catch waves. I had spent some time building up the new skills that I lacked my first time out, but putting this trip together was easier the second time around, and I felt more confident about going out into the water. Kate even decided to join me again, and we planned to spend two full days at Malibu, giving ourselves plenty of time to catch a wave or two. This time around, having learned from the first experience, we also brought our own gear, including full-body wetsuits and boots, and rented the bigger, easier-to-ride soft-top boards.

THE TEST

Kate was very adventurous and had no problem getting right into the ocean. We were already at an advantage, based on what I had learned from my previous attempt, and having a second person there added to my confidence and also just made it a lot more fun. I was able to test what I had prototyped and piloted back on the ground (and in the water) in Minnesota. But this time, I was in the ocean. Right away, I noticed a major difference in my abilities. Not only did I have the knowledge about what was happening in the conditions and with the waves, but I also had the skills to back it up. My paddling was more measured and intentional. I was able to conserve energy between waves and stay relaxed on my board. Being calm allowed me to focus on being in the best position to catch waves. Because I was more confident in my skills, I was able to spend less time and energy managing the conditions and more time using my new skills to surf. I knew that whatever kind of wave came rolling in, there was a good chance I was going to ride it.

THE REWARD

After spending two full days in the water, chasing wave after wave, both Kate and I were satisfied with our efforts and our time spent back in Malibu. We were both able to paddle in and stand up on some waves. Overall, this was a much better outing than my previous first attempt. I still had a lot of room for improvement, but at the end of the last day, I walked out of the water and looked back at the ocean from the beach. I took a few moments to reflect on what I had experienced this second time, and that feeling from my first attempt of being slammed on the beach was gone. The return to Malibu and the formal testing of my new mindset and skills felt as if all the hard work had paid off. I felt forward movement and a sense of progression. Even Malibu didn't seem as big or as dangerous as before. The goal was not to be the best in the water that day, but not to be broken by the conditions—to change how I viewed my skills and how I explored new challenges in the face of risk. This second attempt would serve as the genesis for the changes I would make in my professional life as well.

WORK STORY: PART II

14

EMBRACING THE CONDITIONS

1. MAP: WATCH AND LEARN

SLAMMED IN THE OFFICE

After spending two years meeting with business leaders in a variety of industries and markets, I discovered new insight into their challenges and obstacles. Like the surfer, companies were feeling slammed. They were investing money into sales and marketing programs, but having little impact with their customers. They were struggling in their markets, falling behind competition, and felt held back by their internal processes. The conditions had created a new set of challenges, and business leaders were having a hard time managing this change. I worked with marketing and sales leaders and used the three principles as a way to discuss their challenges. We used the principles as a process to understand the market better, learn new skills, and explore new challenges in the face of risk. By implementing new tactics and strategies, I discovered what successful companies did differently than the status quo and was able to help other organizations solve problems in new and innovative ways as well.

NEW JOURNEY

The three principles of the Ride the Wave Process took business leaders on a new journey to identify opportunities both outside and inside their organizations. The process helped them to focus on specific opportunities they identified and to use new tactics or strategies to build skills and overcome new challenges. As I helped companies work through their challenges, I began using the same principles and process for my own business as well. In helping other companies with their challenges, I saw some of the same obstacles within my own business and realized the impact I could make if I embraced the new concepts that I was helping others implement. I took special note of what I saw that worked and leveraged the new knowledge for my own journey. I was able to watch and learn from the companies that were successful and thwarted the status quo, but also from the organizations that continued to hold onto traditional ideas and were not willing to embrace the new conditions.

EMBRACING THE CONDITIONS

The first area where I noticed customers having success was in their approach to marketing and sales activities—specifically, whether or not they were using outbound or inbound strategies. Most marketing and sales teams were focused on outbound activities only and were not using inbound activities at all or in any kind of strategic way. At the start of our work, leaders felt overwhelmed by the large number of information-sharing platforms and the new technology driven by inbound marketing. As companies began to embrace the conditions and see how customers were finding information as well as buying, however, it was clear that inbound activities would better meet the needs of customers and also align the organization with the decision journey that customers were taking. Based on what I had learned, my first step within my own business was to embrace the changes happening in the market and to get back into the market conditions by using the new inbound strategies.

2. MEASURE: FIND OPPORTUNITIES

SMALL STEPS

As companies took small steps toward using more inbound marketing activities, we discovered which strategies were bringing customers to their websites, motivating them to take action from an email, or triggering a potential customer to pick up the phone and make a call. We measured what was working and what was not, but it was clear that inbound activities were more impactful, created more urgency with customers, and made the companies more confident in what they were doing. For example, one of the companies using inbound activities had increased their website traffic to 300 visits per day. These visitors were also using the new contact form on their site, and we found that this generated better-quality leads for the company's sales teams. This company also focused more of its marketing on inbound activities such as videos and email marketing. The quality of the company's marketing content improved and these tactics helped reach a new audience. Overall, customers responded to the new inbound strategies, which increased year-over-year sales by 25 percent.

JOHN'S JOURNEY

As I began to make progress with inbound marketing strategies for my own business, I looked for ways to continue to leverage what I was learning from my work with other companies and to apply these techniques to my own journey. I had started a new business and was struggling with brand awareness. With all the existing businesses in the market, it was hard to stand out. I would need to be more relevant if I wanted to attract an audience. Even if I had more knowledge or ability, it was still hard to compete with a business that had been around for years, had established clients, and already had a strong reputation in the market. In my work with other companies, I saw that the organizations that focused on producing and delivering good-quality content had the best success with their inbound marketing. These companies had developed content that explored a specific need and used it to help explain to customers how their product or service could solve their problems.

MEASURING UP

Much like the companies I was working with, I tried to develop quality content and to offer suggested solutions to the new challenges. Just like my second surf attempt in Malibu, I was watching and learning what others were doing and then trying to do those things on my own. There was a lot of trial and error involved in this process, but the more I worked with the inbound strategies, the more I started to measure up with the companies that had been doing this type of work for longer periods of time. I used my website to share content through a blog, and then I would repost that content through social media channels or use direct email marketing to share the content within my network. LinkedIn, Twitter, and Facebook were my main social channels, and I sent out a monthly email newsletter via MailChimp. Along with my website, these areas formed a nice three-pronged approach to inbound marketing and became a great way to drive new content to potential customers.

3. PROCESS: REPEATABLE PROCESS

TEST, FAIL, LEARN

Prior to my new journey, I had worked in marketing and sales for most of my career and spent time "carrying a bag" at the customer level. I understood an end-to-end marketing-to-sales process, but had been successful using mostly outbound activities. These inbound activities were new to me, but I wanted to develop these skills to keep up with where the market was going. I created a repeatable process for measuring the success of my inbound activities. The process, much like my surf training, involved testing, failing, and learning. As I continued to work with inbound strategies—and specifically marketing content—I would identify topics that would be relevant to companies and offer a solution to a new challenge. After I had created the content, I posted it to my blog and then my social media channels. I was able to see what topics received the most comments, "likes," or "shares" and could measure my results over a few weeks. I could then use the content that had the best results for my monthly email newsletter, but also repeat the same process and learn as I explored this strategy further.

NEW KNOWLEDGE

Testing content and learning what resonated with my audience was a great way to collect new knowledge. I was able to stay current on sales and marketing topics by creating content, but I was also learning about inbound marketing and what kind of content, posting strategies, and processes worked the best for my business. By using a combination of website and social media analytics, I discovered that the best days of the week to post content were on Tuesdays, Wednesdays, and Thursdays. I had the most LinkedIn activity on Tuesdays at midmorning, the best Facebook responses on Wednesdays in the late afternoon before 5:00 p.m., and the most website visits midweek on Wednesdays as well. I originally started posting daily, but I soon realized that less was more and that I really only needed to create content and share it one to three times per week to be effective. This new knowledge helped me to focus on a posting strategy that targeted specific days of the week, and the process helped me to measure what was working and also made me become more efficient with my time.

NEW SKILLS

The more I worked with an inbound marketing process, the more efficient I became. I focused on specific skills that were strengths, but I also started to build new skills where I had gaps. As I began to narrow down the activities that worked for me, I stuck with the ones where I found success and further honed my skills. I spent less time on activities that did not produce the results I was looking for, which allowed me to use that time to explore new inbound activities that I had not yet tested. As I began to improve with certain skills, others began to present themselves. There was a natural progression through sets of new skills. Much like the surfer building one skill and then exploring another on the next wave, my mindset toward inbound activities started to change, and I proactively began to search for new methods and strategies, even if I thought they were beyond my reach.

PROGRESSION-BASED MINDSET

1. SKILLS: CHANGED MY MINDSET

NEW APPROACH

As I changed my mindset and began to add new inbound marketing skills, I realized that the marketing work I was doing would start to cannibalize what I had traditionally done within sales. Marketing and sales are often seen as "siloed" functional areas, with different goals and each having a set of activities that are separate from one another. As I started to work with clients, I noticed that an organization was either a heavy marketing organization or a heavy sales organization. There were only a handful of companies that were balanced and that invested equal effort in both areas. However, when either marketing or sales was more of a focus than the other, challenges arose within the organization. There was a noticeable misalignment with processes, and the differences made existing problems even worse. Imagine the guy in the gym who does all upper body and no legs. He can bench-press a house, but he would fold like a lawn chair if he had to do a squat. The more I worked with clients on inbound marketing activities, the more I tried to integrate these two functional areas to balance what organizations were doing.

SKILLS ASSESSMENT

The companies that were not integrating their marketing and sales with new skills suffered from misalignment. They worked separately from each other and toward differing goals. I had to work with organizations to change their mindset about skills and also to assess how they thought about their marketing efforts in relation to sales. The biggest discovery was that marketing would need to do more of the lead-generation activities and qualify leads for sales. Marketing was better positioned to identify leads, use lead nurturing to connect with prospects, and qualify leads to be passed along to sales. Email and web activities drove lead scores through marketing and created a qualified lead that could be passed along to sales. This was a challenge at first, since marketing was new to lead generation, but new platforms could help with inbound activities and build a new marketing skill that had not been used before.

COMMITMENT TO CHANGE

As marketing teams started taking on more of the inbound activities, sales teams needed to understand the process, but also be committed to the changes and to the new expectations of their role. Traditional sales strategies had field representatives doing their own lead-generation work. Having marketing take over this aspect of the inbound process would be a major change. Sales would have to trust that the leads coming from marketing would be of a high quality and that it would be a better lead than what they could develop on their own. This change took a commitment from sales, but also a commitment from marketing. Both teams had to trust in the new process and believe that this new approach would be worth the change necessary and not hurt the company in the short or long term. This kind of major change is an example of embracing the conditions and how a progression-based mindset is needed to make sales and marketing efforts more holistic and more impactful.

2. INVEST: WORKED ON SKILLS GAPS

COST OF CHANGE

The more work I did with inbound sales and marketing strategies, the more I found that there was not only a mental aspect of making this change, but a significant financial one as well. For organizations, budgets were often the main obstacle in making any kind of change. If you were working at a midsize or large organization, there was a likelihood you had a decent marketing or sales budget and that you were even looking for ways to spend down that budget rather than lose it the next year. But how and where to allocate budget resources can cause differences of opinions internally, slow down progress, and even prevent the new change from happening. Financial pressures can prevent a team from making a good strategic decision, and thinking about how to spend a budget can be more challenging than the actual decision as to whether or not to make a new change. While sales CRM and email marketing systems have nominal expenses associated with them, there is also a change cost to making a decision that could impact the organization's momentum. Changes in skills can take time and can often disrupt the flow of an organization.

INBOUND PLATFORMS

Using inbound platforms and integrating sales with marketing can bring unforeseen change costs inside the organization and also create up-front financial costs when starting. For the companies that I worked with, the big-ticket items were a website, marketing automation platforms, and sales CRM. Social media and email marketing platforms can be set up at a low cost or no cost at all if they are done in-house, but these areas were more expensive if someone had to be hired from the outside. With my own business, I started with a website, social media platforms, and an email marketing system. I added a blog to my site and used it as one of my main inbound platforms. The blog was free, a great way for posts to show up in organic searches, and also a way to push potential customers to my site, using free content. I also used videos to help explain the Ride the Wave Process and the three principles. I used Vimeo as a posting platform for my digital content, which is another free platform and a great way to deliver content to your audience.

CLOSING THE SALE

The inbound marketing activities I used helped to present content to customers that solved a specific problem or need. Once the visitor had enough information and felt compelled to take action, I created opportunities for the person to connect with my organization. I created an action step that included submitting a project proposal, setting up a workshop, or searching for a related resource. After spending time on my site and becoming more motivated to connect, customers needed a way to take action, and I needed the opportunity to close the sale. The mechanisms included a link and button to a contact form, a link to send an email, and a callout to my direct phone number so that a customer could reach out by phone. The inbound marketing process did most of the heavy lifting and created opportunities for me to act as a concierge and to close the sale.

3. CHANGE: MANAGED THE PROCESS

ALIGNMENT

As I built new inbound marketing and sales skills, I aligned everything I was doing into a single strategic process. I continued to work with the process until I had aligned everything I was doing from a marketing standpoint to what I was doing with my sales. Around this same time, I was working with a healthcare organization and saw how an end-to-end process that was inbound, was integrated, and aligned marketing with sales could support a high-volume strategy. The company had a small sales force and an even smaller marketing team. But because the process was aligned, it was more efficient and the company was able to drive significant sales for a small organization compared to the much larger companies that had massive sales and marketing teams and were only doing outbound activities. After working with this company, I applied what I learned to my own business and created ways to integrate my marketing and sales strategies with my inbound activities.

MARKETING

Once my sales and marketing process was aligned and driven by inbound activities, I did research to identify the industries and companies I wanted to support. I also found the key contacts at those organizations that held sales and marketing roles and created lead lists for my targeting. An easy first step was to invite those leads to connect on LinkedIn and add them to an email-marketing list using MailChimp. Over time, I accumulated thousands of contacts and started to build targeted email-marketing lists by industry. As part of my marketing strategy, I created content that identified the main challenges that my new sales and marketing contacts might be experiencing, specific to their industries. I offered the workshop as a way for my contacts to learn about how to identify and overcome these challenges. The workshop was a great way for potential leads to learn more about how to solve their specific challenges, and for me, the process made it easy to identify participants and create a way for them to connect with my organization.

SALES

The inbound marketing activities drove potential customers to my site who could be interested in the workshop. I used a contact form to collect the names and company information from interested participants. I even had some company leaders call me to set up a time to connect in person or via Skype or GoToMeeting. The workshop strategy worked well because it aligned directly with what I was doing from a content-marketing standpoint. The marketing was driven by content built around the workshop, so when someone did the workshop, it was just a continuation of everything the person had learned while researching on my website, blog, or social media platforms. Doing the workshop allowed me to connect with a new contact in a low-pressure environment since the content was non-branded and meant to be informative. It also provided some credibility, as I was able to display my knowledge about what was changing within sales and marketing and help to uncover the challenges that participants were facing.

RISK AS A COMPASS

1. RISK PLAN: PLANNED FOR RISK

LOWER THE BAR

My new inbound marketing skills began to develop, and I continued to integrate any new marketing strategy with my sales whenever possible. By thinking holistically and as both areas as a single process, I was able to align and streamline much of what I was doing. I found that my marketing and sales efforts were more focused and more effective. After a few months of inbound activities, customers started to reach out to me. That was the biggest change and very different from what I had experienced with my efforts a year earlier. It was a great feeling to have a customer notice my marketing work and ask about my interest in one of their projects. While this was a nice change, I knew that I could not stop exploring inbound strategies. By working with company leaders during workshops, I knew that risk was the single biggest obstacle holding an organization back from trying something new. Organizations would stick with the familiar, even if this meant not achieving the desired results. In order to lower the bar for companies, we started to explore more risk by planning for it.

PLAN FOR RISK

I was able to learn from the companies that were having success and using the principles of the surfer to lower the bar for risk. We used the principles as a process to test new ideas and identify areas of new opportunity. The process allowed us to explore new ideas in a safe environment, and the more we worked through them using the process, the lower the bar was to doing something new. By going through the process, companies had more information and felt more confident in their decisions. A new idea was less of an unknown, and the process produced enough information for us either to spend more time with it or to cut bait and refocus on something else. As an example, an organization used the process to identify where it would allocate its marketing budget for the upcoming year. The process forced the company to think hard about what aspects of marketing and sales it would invest in further and if there were new areas to commit to that the company had avoided previously because of the risks.

RISK VS. PROGRESSION

The biggest challenge for me was how to take on new risk and balance it with how I was progressing with building new skills and abilities. Just like my surf training from the previous chapter, my progression was limited by the amount of risk I was willing to explore. The more risk I took on, the more I progressed. The more I tried to push toward new skills, the more my professional world began to open up and create new opportunities for my business. I learned that the risk-taking process was not about risk for the sake of risk or pushing myself beyond what I was capable of skill-wise, but trying to systematically work through a progression of steps to go somewhere new. Planning for the risk and scoping it out on the front end helped me take a progressive approach to what I was doing, and I was able to move forward faster because of it.

2. PROTOTYPE: TRIED NEW THINGS

PROTOTYPE

In exploring risk and using the Ride the Wave Process and principles to explore new strategies, I continued to look for opportunities to test what I was doing. I tend to be the type of person who pushes for change and tries new things, even when a change is not necessary. On most occasions, things work out, and the risk usually pays off. But there are occasions (like trying ocean surfing for the first time) where I try something new and end up looking a fool. That's okay with me. I would rather be like the surfer who tries to pull off a technical maneuver and fails versus the surfer who does the same old trick and receives no enjoyment from it. I think it's better to have tried and failed than not to have tried at all. As I continued to take that approach with my business, I prototyped new ideas and strategies in order to find out what would work, but also to lower the risk I was taking. We tend to think of prototyping as an approach to product design, but there's no reason we can't take this same approach within business. I actually found this very effective when the risks were at their highest.

PILOT

An area where I would try to prototype new ideas and strategies was with my messaging. Some of the best feedback I have received has often been from moments where I prototyped an idea, just to see how it would work. Another way to see if a new idea will work is to create a situation where you can pilot it. I also tried to pilot new ideas during webinars and workshops. For Ride the Wave workshops, I preferred to do them face-to-face, but there were times, due to travel or schedules, where I would do them via Skype or GoToMeeting. For the online workshops, I pilot-tested new presentations and my new messaging. I was able to go through the presentation and see how the flow of the talk worked with the audience. Participants could also be involved by asking questions, and I could receive instant feedback on an idea or strategy. But in this format, I was able to pilot new ideas and did not have the pressures I would normally have when trying to do something new.

TEST

As I prototyped new messaging and piloted online programs, I was able to see what was working and what was not. In most situations, there were some risks, including things not working or receiving less of a response, but I planned ahead and did what I could to lower the risks. It helped to know how something that worked in practice might work in reality and not just in theory. As I tested the messaging for the Ride the Wave workshop and figured out what the triggers were for marketing and sales leaders, I could focus on the tactics that were bringing success and put more focus on those areas during presentations. Once I knew the triggers that participants responded to, I created a separate workshop page on my website with the triggers and then used sponsored ads that directed traffic to the workshop page. I found that there were certain keywords such as "strategy workshop" and "marketing strategy" that worked well. Prototyping my messaging and doing pilot presentations helped me with this process and made the keyword tests and ads more effective.

3. REWARD: TOOK ON RISK

NEW VIEW

After spending over two years working with hundreds of business leaders within marketing and sales, I saw firsthand the challenges they were facing. They encountered new conditions, had to identify and learn new skills, and faced a new level of professional risk they had not experienced before. It was clear that a new process for overcoming these challenges was needed. Based on what I learned from the companies I was working with and applying what I learned to my own business, I developed the three principles of the surfer and the Ride the Wave Process. The process helped companies to create a new view of problems or challenges, a new perspective as to what the organization thought was possible, and a new path for organizations to find success. The new view for the organizations that embraced the conditions, changed their mindset, and added new skills was a new view of how to explore risk as well as to see risk as less of a threat and more of an opportunity or the new compass for success.

NEW PROCESS

Companies used the Ride the Wave Process for identifying opportunities to create strategic growth and as a guide for navigating new risk. The process helped to create a new roadmap for achieving market success and fundamentally changed the way the organizations did business. I created the Ride the Wave Process for myself, but also as a process to help companies manage these new conditions and to think about marketing and sales in a new way. Business leadership used the process to integrate sales and marketing processes and aligned each functional area around shared goals. The new process helped marketing and sales explore risk by building new skills and capabilities that better aligned with the customers in their markets. By using the process, I helped companies solve challenges in three ways: 1) Supported companies as they developed new sales and marketing strategies 2) Assisted companies with the development of new systems and processes that were more efficient and effective 3) Gave leadership a new way to solve challenges and learn how to ride the wave on their own.

NEW REALITY

Leaders who used the process helped to create a new reality for their organizations. They were more confident in their abilities to identify new opportunities and discovered white space in their established markets by going through the process. The Ride the Wave Process helped me to realize that products and services are more than just that; they should be unique brands that are customer-driven, solve problems, and differentiate themselves from the status quo. I used the Ride the Wave Process to assist companies as they overcame the new challenges within sales and marketing, but I also created a new reality for myself during the process. I developed new sales and marketing skills and capabilities, but I also changed how I fundamentally thought about business and what I was capable of doing within it. The reward for taking on this new risk was the creation of my new reality and the new perspective that I will bring to my work and personal life.

CONCLUSION: THE UNIVERSAL "STOKE"

15

SURF STOKE

1. PREPARATION

TRAINING

The concept of *riding the wave* is a universal lesson, and while it's derived from surfing, it can be applied to business as well as to any aspect of life. The three principles can be a guide for overcoming any new challenge, and the process is a way to navigate the new challenges we face and to overcome the internal obstacles that we encounter when trying to change who we are and what we do. Regardless of whether we are talking about surfing, business, or our personal lives, the principles and process are a way to create change. When surfers ride a wave, they have a certain feeling. Surfers refer to this feeling as "stoke" or the feeling you have after accomplishing something of significance on a wave. This feeling of stoke is universal and can also be experienced in business or in our personal lives. In order for surfers to experience stoke, they go through a process of preparation to learn how to embrace the conditions and prepare themselves for whatever risks they encounter in the water. I think we do the same when preparing for business-related endeavors or otherwise.

LEARNING

Surfers, like any athlete, will prepare by going through a training process that breaks down each aspect of what they will need to do in the water. There is a process of learning and building new skills, but also understanding the conditions that they will be putting themselves in. Surfers learn each time they paddle out on their board, since the conditions are always changing and the knowledge needed to surf is continually evolving as well, keeping them on their toes, literally and figuratively. This type of constant learning has focused the sport on progression and always moving forward. Whether it's learning more about the ocean, a new surf sport, or new tricks, having a progression-based mindset toward training and preparation is vital to a surfer's success within the sport. Without that mindset of embracing the conditions and learning new skills, surfers would struggle and expose themselves to greater risk.

PROGRESSION

As surfers prepare by training and learning more about the conditions, the idea of progression is always at the forefront of what they do. Surfers have a mindset that is wired to think about whether or not their skills will be suited for the conditions or if there's something new they need to learn how to do, using what they have learned to take on tougher and more challenging conditions. In order to achieve that feeling of stoke or accomplishment, surfers focus on progression to get there. Progression is what drives the surfers toward stoke, and that feeling cannot be achieved without it. As surfers progress, they achieve new levels of success within their sport and new levels of stoke as well. Progression leads to that sense of accomplishment, but it is achieved from preparation, practice, and trying to do things that are new.

2. PRACTICE

THE MOMENT

The surf stoke is a result of preparation and practice. It's that feeling of being in the moment, *riding the wave*, and feeling the success of accomplishing a new trick, cutback, or aerial maneuver. Having prepared for this moment, the surfer lets the training take over and goes more by feel than anything else. The surfer practiced for this moment by building new skills and capabilities, systemically at building new skills over time and then putting those skills into practice. The moment can often be short and fleeting for the surfer, but that small taste of success, even if just for a few seconds, can be all the reward the surfer needs. It's the culmination of practice and preparation coming together in a single moment to give the surfer the reward he or she has been working toward. Surfers mentally prepare themselves for this moment and align their physical abilities with what they have set out to do in their mind.

MIND AND BODY

The moment the surfer catches the wave and feels the stoke, it's a moment when the mind and body have come together to accomplish a goal. The surfer has set out to catch a wave and has prepared for the moment by putting together a mental roadmap of what to accomplish, and then physically executing on the plan. The feeling represents a synergy of intentional and thoughtful planning with physical preparation and training. All of this work and effort culminate for a moment of spontaneity on an unpredictable wave. Hours of planning, training, and preparing go into moments like this, with the final step focused on execution, making that moment a surfer catches a wave and the resulting feeling of stoke even more incredible. For the surfer, the rarity of that moment and connecting the mind and body to nature is what makes the sport of surfing so unique and the surf stoke so elusive.

FINDING SUCCESS

After riding a wave, there is an instant feeling of success and accomplishment. That moment when surfers know they have pulled off a new trick or accomplished something risky is all part of the stoke. That feeling of success is tied back to the effort made in planning, preparing, and training. The surfer knows that the work was directed at a specific goal and that the goal was accomplished: thinking about a trick, planning for it, visualizing it, and doing the work necessary to pull it off. The stoke leads to a cycle of satisfaction that fuels the surfer to search for that feeling again, to use it as fuel to build new skills and abilities through progression. That sense of accomplishment is what the surfer has worked for and will continue to strive for each time he or she paddles out. A feeling of success in the moment and stoke from riding the wave.

3. PROGRESSION

CALM

After riding the wave, the surf stoke moves from a feeling of euphoria in the moment to a sense of resolution and calm, as if the surfer had been experiencing a problem, and it was solved by simply catching a wave. A feeling of calm comes over the surfer as if the volume has been turned down in the rest of the world—the finalization of a frantic moment to the gradual coming down from the experience. This calm is also a sign of progression for the surfers. It means something challenging was accomplished and gives the surfer a reason to try again. When the surfer is able to move forward through various tests and failures, to reach that point of accomplishment and have that feeling, it fuels the surfer's motivation to continue the progress for the new challenges to come.

MOTIVATION

During the calm, surfers will replay the moment in their head and reflect on how they were able to achieve their success. This fuels their motivation for more and helps motivate surfers to think about what should come next. Surfers are motivated by this sense of accomplishment and driven to think beyond what just happened to something new. They have renewed motivation to try something new and are already thinking about the next ride. The mind of the surfer is based in progression, so success is a strong motivator and starts the process of working toward the next goal. After working through the process of planning for a new trick and accomplishing it, the surfer does not stop there. Instead, the surfer begins the process all over again. For the surfer, the stoke is motivating and always fuels what will come next.

THE PROCESS

This process is repeatable for the surfer and helps them to keep building new skills over time. Surfers know how to leverage progression on wave after wave, and they can quickly move through a series of tricks and challenges to improve their surfing. The surfers that have mastered the process of building skills through progression will not stop and bask in their accomplishments. The process for the surfer is about accomplishing something and then building on it toward something new, using a repeatable process to build upon their accomplishments instead of resting on them. Most sports are built on static skills or abilities that change very little over time. Surfers are continually raising the bar to surf a bigger wave, do more spins in the air, or catch a longer ride. A process built on progression is more challenging, and there is more fluctuation in terms of success and failure. The stakes are also far greater because of the risks. Surfers have created a blueprint for overcoming new challenges and created a way for business leaders to do the same.

BUSINESS STOKE

1. PLANNING

MINDSET

For business leaders, the surfer's stoke and that feeling of riding the wave is similar to when a marketing campaign goes viral—it's just described in different terms. The process to get there is the same, but the context is different. The surf conditions are very different from the business environments we work in, but the principles of the surfer can be applied to the work that what we do every day. The way to achieve that feeling is to apply the three principles when faced with challenging business situations. Just like the surfer who embraces the conditions, adopts a progression-based mindset, and uses risk as a compass, marketing and sales leaders need to do the same in order to find success. Business leadership must face new challenging business conditions and then use a progression-based mindset to ride the new waves in challenging markets. Having the right mindset and thinking strategically about what you are doing will help you to find success.

STRATEGIC THINKING

When embracing the new conditions, business leaders will need to think strategically about what they want to accomplish and how they will overcome their new challenges. Thinking strategically is about identifying the business factors that will impact what you want to do and using strategic planning to manage the change you are working toward. Using a progression-based mindset and thinking strategically, just like the surfer thinking about trick progression, will help you to create a mental roadmap from where you are to where you want to be. It can be difficult to keep an open mind while you are trying to analyze or evaluate new market situations, but strategic thinking, much like a surfer planning his or her journey from the shore, will help you to make smart decisions about how to plan for new risk and make progressive improvement toward your goals.

IMPROVEMENT

Keeping an open mind and thinking strategically will naturally help you to improve on what you are doing. You will have to progress and do things that are new, but it will feel more natural if improvements are made using a strategic process that you are managing. If you keep yourself open to new ideas and push yourself to evaluate your level of improvement, there is a natural progression of skill and ability that will develop. Planning for the risks involved with making these changes and then taking action will help you improve, even if you experience failure from time to time. Making changes in yourself professionally will take focus, perseverance, and the motivation to execute, even when it feels tough or when the stakes are high. Executing on your plans will help fuel your motivation, and like the surfer, you will experience the professional stoke of accomplishing your goals.

2. EXECUTION

FOCUS

For the business professional, achieving the business stoke requires planning and execution. After the business professional has strategically planned what to accomplish and created the plan to get there, execution of the new initiative will require focus, perseverance, and a high level of commitment. Planning will guide the sales and marketing professional on this journey and keep the focus on the objective of accomplishing a new goal. However, business leaders will be especially challenged to stay focused in the new conditions and will be pulled in multiple directions because of the distractions competing for their attention. Focus and discipline will be required since what you are trying to do is new and untested. Not fully committing 100 percent of your attention can lead to failure and expose you to risk. When taking on any new challenge with the process, know that your attention will need to be focused on the task at hand to *ride the wave*.

PERSEVERANCE

Focused attention on your new initiatives will give you a better chance of finding success, but will also help you stick to the process and work through it to the end. Just like the surfer, you will be progressing toward a new goal and will need to persevere in order to accomplish it. You will need to persevere and not stray from the process or from what you originally set out to do. Riding the wave requires focus and the willingness to persevere through the process, even when obstacles arise and setbacks occur. You will need to make multiple attempts at what you're doing because it will be new, it will be hard, and it will be in direct opposition to what you have traditionally done. You will need to persevere with the immediate task, but also with the entire process. This will take time and a full commitment if you plan to *ride the wave*. Focus and perseverance will help you through the stages of the new change, but your commitment to the process will move you forward to the next steps.

COMMITMENT

As you start to work through the process and experience both success and failure, your commitment to the process will be needed to achieve success. The surfer knows and understands that progression happens over time and that, while stoke is rare and fleeting, it's still very possible to achieve on a consistent basis if you stick with the process. Commitment comes from the focus and attention that you give to the process, but also from the commitment you make to yourself and the organization. Surfers commit to the process to progressively build their skills and capabilities, but they also commit in the moment and to the wave they're trying to catch. Hesitation in the ocean can get you killed, and hesitation in business can cause professional harm and your organization to suffer. Without a commitment to change and the process, marketing and sales professionals will expose themselves to risk and miss out on the opportunity to find success.

3. SUCCESS

WAVE OF SUCCESS

As you go through the process of *riding the wave*, you will start to feel the natural momentum build from your efforts. You will start to notice changes occurring in how you think and what you do. Through commitment and perseverance, the three principles will help you to catch a wave and create a pathway to success. Once you have found momentum in your market, your new initiatives and strategies will start to build like a wave. You will find that achieving new initiatives is easier, you will have more insight into customer needs, and you will work through a progressive set of steps like the surfer moving through a set of tricks on the board. The stoke comes from that feeling of setting out to achieve something new, building a plan to accomplish it, and using the momentum you have generated to find success.

GOING VIRAL

The closest thing that business leaders have to the feeling of stoke is when a product, service, or strategy goes viral. Going viral is when a new company or product becomes a household name or is known by a majority of people. A marketing ad or campaign can go from being unknown to a mainstream audience in a short period of time and almost overnight. Catching a wave in surfing and feeling that stoke is similar to when something goes viral in business. If you think about the commercials or ads that have gone viral, there's something unique and novel about them. It could be the song or the actor, but it all seems to come together naturally and almost out of nowhere. That's what riding the wave and stoke is like for the surfer. A wave builds up on the horizon out of nowhere, and the surfer is in the right place at the right time, has prepared for this moment, and is able to successfully ride it into shore— just like the ad that connects with an audience at the right time with the right message and solves the exact customer need at the right time.

A BIGGER PURPOSE

As marketing and sales professionals, there is more to our work than just getting customers to buy products or services. There is a bigger purpose than brands and a bigger reason we all do what we do. We chase the professional stoke and achieve that feeling of going viral or knowing that you put together a great sales or marketing plan and that it was you that made it happen. For professionals, the bigger purpose for them personally is to achieve that satisfaction or feeling of success, but our duty or our responsibility as business leaders is to transfer that feeling to our customers—giving the people who are buying our products and services that stoke or that feeling of riding a wave when they use what we have created in their everyday lives. Customers can become very attached to brands, and that product or service can create an important connection for them. Customers are inseparable from the brands they love, they can become a part of who they are, and a product can become an important part of their daily lives. Our responsibility is to work to achieve that feeling for ourselves, but also to do what we can to give that feeling back to our customers.

LIFE STOKE

1. EMBRACE THE CONDITIONS

NEW CONDITIONS

The Ride the Wave analogy is used to make sense of the new and changing conditions within business. Marketing and sales professionals will need to embrace the conditions, adopt a progression-based mindset, and use risk as a compass in order to achieve success. The Ride the Wave Process is about using the natural momentum within markets to find success rather than resisting or pushing back against these strong and powerful changes. The analogy not only works for business, but it also works as an example for everyday life. Regardless of your skill level, education level, or professional or non-professional background, anyone can use the three principles in their own lives and overcome any new obstacle or challenge. Ask yourself, what is the situation I am in and what are the conditions that are holding me back? Embracing the conditions is first about understanding the context in which you are in and then deciding what the desired outcome is that you want to achieve.

NEW VISION

After you understand the conditions, you need to understand what is required in order to make this change happen. Without knowing what the conditions are and not understanding them through experience, you will be planning for change without knowing the challenges you will face. In order to set a new vision, you need to get out there, see what the challenges are, and identify where your gaps will be. You can then start to create your vision of what it will look like for you to accomplish your goals and what new skills you will need in order to do so. You will need to be bold enough first to test the waters and see what the conditions are like. Get out there and experience them firsthand because you will never understand them from the shore. Once you have your plan in place and your journey mapped out, you will need to commit to the process and start your new journey. This new journey will be challenging because you will be learning new skills as you go, but let the vision pull you through the process and just commit to taking the first step on your new journey.

NEW JOURNEY

When you begin the journey, think of it as a long-term process, not a short-term one. Real and significant change takes time. Especially when that change involves a new mindset, new skills, and a new process. Know that the road is long, bumpy, and full of numerous twists and turns. You have tested the conditions and know the gaps you need to close, so stick to the process you have established and work toward slowly building your new skills through a progression. We tend to look at making a change like we are cramming for a test. We try to do too much in a short period of time. The results are usually mixed, and we give up because we have not given the new change the proper time to develop. Progression as it relates to your skills and abilities will take more time than you think since you are building new habits as well. This process takes time and a mindset based on slowly building new capabilities over time while planning for what new skills you need to develop next.

2. PROGRESSION-BASED MINDSET

PROGRESSION

When you change your mindset from thinking about your skills and capabilities in terms of being static, and instead as being more fluid, you have an open rather than a fixed mindset. You are more willing to expose yourself to opportunities that are new. Rather than being closed off to new opportunities in your life, such as a new job, a new city, or a new partner, you start to think about your approach to these decisions as more of a process or an evolution. You are proactively making decisions instead of making reactive ones. Riding the wave and having a mindset toward progression is about asking yourself, "How will I make these changes and what new skills do I need to do it?" Progression changes how you view what is happening in your world and how you are responding to these factors, which also helps you to manage and meet the demands of changing conditions better. It's a mindset based on pursuing what is new and leaving the old behind.

NEW SKILLS

Once you have identified your new skills and your mindset is based in progression, you will need to push yourself to do things that are uncomfortable and new. You will need to start working on the skills you planned for and focus on what you need to change in order to close the gaps to get there. A mindset of progression will, in a positive way, force you to start making changes and decisions that support your new vision. "If I'm going to do this, what will I need to change about myself? What do I need to do differently, and how can I start creating this new world I want to exist in?" These questions will help you determine which new skills and capabilities to build and help move you from where you currently are to where you want to go, but in a focused and disciplined manner. As you begin to add and develop the new skills, the context you are working in will need to change as well. It's easy to start doing something differently and to make small artificial changes, but the larger changes that you are working toward will need to be supported by a new context as well.

NEW JOURNEY

The new journey will begin when you have created a new context to manage the change. You will need to drive the change yourself, but be supported by others who will also help make the new journey possible. You will find that some people who share your progressive mindset will be supportive with your process to change. Others, however, will want to keep the context the same and not let you become the new you. They will be comfortable with the old you, the old context, and the old way things were. They will see your push for change as a threat. Working to change the context for yourself will be important, but it will also change the context for others as well. It will be important to recognize this as it happens and to be open about what you are doing with others so that they will see why the change is necessary and that it's ultimately not about them, but about you and your new journey. This will be important as you move from planning to building your world. Be prepared to work others through the process just as you are doing the same for yourself.

3. RISK AS A COMPASS

REGRET

As you begin to change your mindset and develop your new skills and capabilities, you will need to free yourself from the risks associated with what you are doing and act as well as live without regret. You will most certainly make mistakes, ruffle some feathers, and do things that just simply fall flat. That's part of the process and the important part of progression: testing what you think might work, having success or experiencing failure, learning from it, and moving forward because of it. Ask yourself, "What risks am I willing to take in order to achieve this?" Are you okay feeling embarrassed if you mess up? Can you accept bad results and not regret those decisions? You will need to test ideas in practice and then in reality. As much as you try to plan for challenges in advance, things will sometimes go sideways. Prototyping ideas, piloting them, and testing are not just strategies for business, but they can be applied to any aspect of your life and any challenge no matter how big or how small. You have no regrets when you approach challenges this way, and this mindset will give you the freedom to make bold new decisions.

FREEDOM

When you explore things in your personal and professional life without regret and with a process that minimizes risk, you are more willing to accept failure. You can create a new sense of freedom with what you do. Instead of changes or challenges being an all-or-nothing approach, you have a way to overcome obstacles that creates a sense of new freedom and confidence to try things that were once perceived as risky. This new dynamic changes your ideas around what is possible, and there is a new sense of freedom with the way you live. Risk is viewed in terms of what is next, instead of something to be avoided. Over time, you will build new skills that will support you and bring you success, but there will be others that come and go as you embrace the changing conditions. Know that it is okay to progress this way and that it will help you feel less pressure and more confidence as well as make you more likely to enjoy the risks.

UNIVERSAL STOKE

Ride the Wave is a strategic planning process for business, but it provides a universal lesson for anyone who wants to change, do something new, and not let risk dictate choices or success. During my personal journey through this process, I learned that with the new conditions and changes in sales and marketing, I had to embrace the conditions, change my mindset about how I developed new skills, and just get out there and explore risk to do something new. The new knowledge I acquired is powerful, and the process I developed has helped me find a new kind of stoke in both my personal and professional life. What I learned is a universal lesson that anyone can use to take on risk and overcome new challenges. There has never been a time when we've had more access to people, technology, information, and resources. Things are moving faster than ever, but this is no time to stand on the shore. It's important that we all get out there and ride our own personal and professional waves.

"The important thing in the Olympic Games
is not the winning but the taking part.
The important thing in life is not the triumph
but the struggle."

—*Pierre De Coubertin*
(Founder of the Olympic Games)

SURF TERMS:

AERIAL – A maneuver where the surfer catches air above the top of the wave

BAIL – Jumping off a surfboard to avoid a wipeout

BARNEY – An inexperienced surfer or someone who is not good at surfing

BARREL – When the wave is breaking and makes a hollow tube

CAUGHT INSIDE – When a surfer is too far in and the waves are breaking

CHARGING – A surfer who is aggressively surfing a wave

CLEAN UP SET – A set of waves that break before and "clean up" the line-up

DUCK DIVE – Diving under an oncoming wave when paddling out

GROM – A young or inexperienced surfer

HANG TEN – Riding a longboard with both feet directly on the nose of the board

IMPACT ZONE – The area where the waves are breaking

JEFFREYS BAY – A South African surf break that is one of the best in the world

JAWS – Pe'ahi, on the island of Maui, is a big wave surf break known as Jaws

KOOK – A beginner or someone who is not very good at surfing

LEASH – The cord that is attached from your leg to your surfboard

LINE-UP – The area where surfers wait for waves

LOCALISM – When surfers are territorial about waves, not letting others surf them

MAVERICKS – A famous big wave spot off the northern coast of California

OUTSIDE – The area further out and beyond the line-up

POP-UP – The move a surfer makes to go from a lying to a standing position

STOKED – Being happy or excited to go surfing, or the feeling of catching a wave

SURFRIDER BEACH – A famous surf spot in Malibu

TEAHUPOO – A surf spot near Tahiti known for big waves

TOMBSTONING – When a surfer is pushed underwater, but the leash keeps the board at the surface, making the board stick out of the water like a tombstone

TUBE – Like a barrel, this is the hollow area where the wave is breaking

WIPEOUT – Falling off your board or getting slammed by a wave

ACKNOWLEDGEMENTS:

I would like to thank my family, friends, and professional connections that helped me during the planning, writing, and publishing process. There is no way I would have been able to do this on my own, so I appreciate everyone that helped me make this book a reality.

Kate Doman, Chuck Wessinger, Louise Wessinger, Nick Wessinger, Chris Doman, Phyllis Doman, Dan Stefaniak, Joey Lomicky, Sally Power, John Sandhal, Sally Koering-Zimney, Megan Junius, Jennifer Gilhoi, Tim Krieg, Scott Welle, Jenna Bauer, Mark Anderson, Tyler Smith, Wise Ink Creative Publishing, Dara Beevas, Patrick Maloney, Amy Quale, Rosanne Cheng, Alison Watts, Ceciley Pund, Dan Pitts and anyone else that may have contributed informally during the process.

Thank you!
John

BIBLIOGRAPHY

Delmulle, Bart, Brett Grehan, and Vikas Sagar. "Building Marketing and Sales Capabilities to Beat the Market." *McKinsey Quarterly*, March 2015. http://www.mckinsey. com/business-functions/marketing-and-sales/our-insights/ building-marketing-and-sales-capabilities-to-beat-the-market.

Hatami, Homayoun, Kevin McLellan, Candace Lun Plotkin, and Patrick Shulze. "Six Steps to Transform Your Marketing and Sales Capabilities." *McKinsey Quarterly*, March 2015. http://www.mckinsey.com/business-functions/marketing-and-sales/our-insights/six-steps-to-transform-your-marketing-and-sales-capabilities.

Lingqvist, Oskar, Candace Lun Plotkin, and Jennifer Stanley. "Do You Really Understand How Your Business Customers Buy?" *McKinsey Quarterly*, February 2015. http://www. mckinsey.com/business-functions/marketing-and-sales/ our-insights/do-you-really-understand-how-your-business-customers-buy.